William J Foy

D1082700

OLD TESTAMENT STUDIES

Volume 1

The Maccabean Revolt

Anatomy
of a
Biblical Revolution

by

Daniel J. Harrington, S.J.

Michael Glazier
Wilmington, Delaware

ABOUT THE AUTHOR

Daniel J. Harrington, S.J., is professor of New Testament at Weston School of Theology in Cambridge, Massachusetts, and general editor of *New Testament Abstracts.* He earned his Ph.D. in Near Eastern Languages and Literatures at Harvard University in 1970. He has written regularly for the leading scholarly journals; and among his books published by Michael Glazier, Inc. are: *Interpreting the New Testament: A Practical Guide; Interpreting the Old Testament: A Practical Guide; Light of All Nations: Studies on the Church in New Testament Research; The New Testament: A Bibliography;* and he is editorial consultant and participant in the translation and annotation of *The Aramaic Bible (The Targums).*

The Scripture quotations contained herein are from the Revised Standard Version Bible, copyright 1946, 1952, 1971 by the Division of Christian Education of the National Council of the Churches of Christ in the USA, and are used by permission.

First published in 1988 by Michael Glazier, Inc., 1935 West Fourth Street, Wilmington, Delaware 19805.

Copyright ©1988 by Michael Glazier, Inc. All rights reserved.

Library of Congress Catalog Card Number: 88-81307
International Standard Book Number:
   OLD TESTAMENT STUDIES: 0-89453-654-0
   The Maccabean Revolt: 0-89453-655-9

Typography by Eileen Williams.
Printed in the United States of America.

In Memory of My Mother

Mary A. Harrington (1912-88)

Contents

1

Introduction:
Canonical and Historical Settings

This study of the Maccabean revolt as a biblical revolution comes out of many years of teaching theological students about the principal literary sources for that revolution and the events described in them. From these years of teaching I have come away with two convictions: These books (Daniel, 1 Maccabees, and 2 Maccabees) are difficult to read, and they tell a fascinating and important story. I intend this volume as a simple introduction to the biblical books of the Maccabean revolt and to the story that they tell.

Daniel and 1—2 Maccabees tend to be neglected in introductions to the Old Testament and in surveys of Old Testament history. They usually come at the end of such courses and textbooks, when energy is low and interest is waning. Specialists in the Old Testament tend to regard these books as "late" and therefore of secondary importance. New Testament specialists regard them as "early" and beyond the scope of their background studies.

Besides their unfavorable place in the canon and biblical history, these books are neglected because they are hard to read. The stories in the first part of the book of Daniel are charming and duly famous. Who has not heard of the idol with clay feet, or Daniel in the lion's den, or the handwriting on the wall? But trying to say what these wonderful stories meant in their historical settings is more difficult. The visions contained in the book of Daniel have fascinated interpreters for many centuries, and the most amazing scenarios have been read out of them. If those visions are to be rescued from the wild imaginings of electronic evangelists, they must first be viewed against the historical background in which they were originally produced—Jewish history in the second century B.C. First and Second Maccabees seem initially to be easier books than Daniel. But even enthusiastic readers find them hard to finish. One problem is the very unfamiliarity of the story that they tell in such detail. First Maccabees traces a Jewish dynasty over a forty-year period in the mid-second century B.C. It is full of unfamiliar names of persons and places, as well as institutions and customs rooted in the Hellenistic world. Second Maccabees begins with apparently extraneous material sure to discourage the beginner. When the real story starts in chapter three, the reader may be at first swept up in what is clearly a well-told story only to encounter rough going again once the battles begin.

In addition to their unfavorable place in the study of the Bible and their difficult content, these books are sometimes neglected for theological reasons. Many Christians and Jews today are embarrassed by the "militarism" of the Maccabees. They find their "warrior religion" primitive and dangerous. Those advocates of "liberation theology" who find a place for military action in responding to evils flowing from unjust political and social structures tend so to focus on the exodus from Egypt as to ignore the Maccabean revolt.

Despite their difficulty, these books (and related sources) tell a fascinating and important story. The story is fascinating when we let it unfold according to its historical sequence. My teaching experience has taught me that the order adopted in chapters two (Daniel), three (2 Maccabees), and four (1 Maccabees) of this book is pedagogically most helpful. Daniel begins with relatively familiar stories and proceeds to the visions, thereby engaging the imagination and plunging the reader into the wild excitement generated by the threat from Antiochus IV Epiphanes. Second Maccabees supplies information about the major figures in the events leading up to the Maccabean revolt. What is referred to by allusion in Daniel and summarized in the first chapter of 1 Maccabees is told at length and with some clarity in 2 Maccabees. Since 2 Maccabees focuses on the Jerusalem temple and takes the story down only to 161 B.C., 1 Maccabees can be used to supplement the other sources where parallels exist and then to continue the story down to the time of John Hyrcanus (134-104 B.C.). This order for reading the principal documents regarding the Maccabean revolt is pedagogical in intent. It does not embody a firm decision about their order of composition. Nor should it give the impression that one can simply put the three books together, and hope that what emerges is the history of the Maccabean revolt. In fact, a special emphasis in our presentations of Daniel, 2 Maccabees, and 1 Maccabees will be the distinctive angles from which their authors viewed the events that they described. A large part of the fascination of the Maccabean revolt lies in the availability of multiple sources that can be compared and evaluated.

The story is important when we study it from the perspective of Jewish history (chapter five). At the beginning of the events narrated in these books, the Jews of early second-century B.C. Palestine constituted a small client people emerging out of a hundred years of Egyptian (Ptolemaic) control and recently plunged into Syrian (Seleucid) control. Jerusalem at this time has been described as a "sleepy" temple city. At the end of the Maccabean revolt the Jews of Palestine were an independent people, with their own high priest and ruler, allied to the Romans but not yet under their direct control. No one would have predicted such an amazing twist in Jewish history at the outset. No one can deny that the Maccabean revolt changed the course of Jewish history and contributed thereby to the development of early Christianity.

While the focus of this book is on the principal literary sources for the Maccabean revolt (Daniel, 2 Maccabees, 1 Maccabees), attention is also given in chapter six to other ancient sources that may refer or allude to events that took place during the Maccabean revolt. The impression of diversity within Judaism that one takes away from the primary sources is reinforced by looking at the more peripheral sources. That fascinating experience of comparing multiple sources for a single event is enriched by studying those other sources in their historical context.

If the course of Jewish and Christian history changed as a

result of the Maccabean revolt, so did the course of Jewish and Christian theology (see chapter seven). Through the centuries the example of Judas and his brothers has inspired religious people to take up arms against unjust oppressors and persecutors of religion. The stories of the Maccabean martyrs have enabled Jews and Christians to face death in a noble and heroic way. Whatever the origins and roots of apocalyptic thought may have been, it is in the book of Daniel and other writings of the Maccabean period that we have our best examples of Jewish apocalypticism. Two essential features of apocalyptic thinking associated most clearly with the Maccabean revolt are the resurrection of the dead and the figure of the Son of Man. The official commemoration of the dedication of the Jerusalem temple by Judas and his companions is the festival of Hanukkah, a relatively minor Jewish feast but very important in the USA and Europe as the "Jewish equivalent" of Christmas.

This book is intended as a simple introduction to a complicated but fascinating and important story. To use it effectively, one should have access to a modern translation accompanied with brief notes. I suggest the Revised Standard Version and will use that fairly literal translation in my own presentation.

This book aims to lead the reader first through a careful reading of Daniel, 2 Maccabees, and 1 Maccabees. Then it seeks to introduce some related historical, literary, and theological material. At the end of the book the reader should be ready to proceed to the next level of study: commentaries, historical investigations, and scholarly monographs. Therefore I have provided a kind of road map for further study by way of an annotated bibliography.

Canonical Setting

Before situating Daniel, 1 Maccabees, and 2 Maccabees in their ancient historical setting, we need to set them within the canon of Scripture. The canonical status of the book of Daniel is acknowledged by Catholics, Protestants, and Jews alike. Protestant and Jewish Bibles present as the book of Daniel the translation of the text in the Hebrew Bible—the twelve chapters that have come down to us in Hebrew and Aramaic. Catholic Bibles include as part of the canonical book three additional pieces: the Prayer of Azariah and Song of the Three Young Men; Susanna; and Bel and the Dragon. These additional pieces were part of the Greek Bible tradition (the Septuagint), though one or more may have been composed in Hebrew or Aramaic. In this book we treat as the book of Daniel only the twelve chapters contained in the Hebrew Bible. This decision is not a judgment against the canonical status of the three additional pieces. It is merely a literary-historical judgment taken out of a desire to understand better what was going on in second century B.C. Jewish history. Our interest in Daniel here is as a witness to the events that comprised the Maccabean revolt. The text of Daniel most appropriate to that purpose is the combination of Hebrew and Aramaic stories and visions found in the Hebrew Bible and translated in versions of the Bibles produced under Jewish and Protestant auspices. Many such Bibles (Revised Standard Version, New English Bible, Good News Bible) include the additions to Daniel in an appendix with the other "Apocrypha."

The canonical status of 1 Maccabees and 2 Maccabees is even more complicated. The canon of Old Testament writings traditional in Catholicism includes all the books of the Hebrew Bible along with seven more books that were part of the Greek Bible tradition (and the Latin tradition also): Judith, Tobit, Baruch, Sirach/Ecclesiasticus, Wisdom of Solomon, 1 Maccabees, and 2 Maccabees. Also included are some additions to Esther and Daniel. The additional books in the Catholic canon are sometimes called the Apocrypha ("hidden books") or the Deuterocanonicals ("second canon"). The canons of various Orthodox churches contain material beyond even what appears in the Catholic canon.

First and Second Maccabees belong to the Catholic (and Orthodox) canon of Sacred Scripture. Protestants and Jews sometimes refer to these books as the Apocrypha or the Deuterocanonicals. As a Catholic biblical scholar, I am assuming that the two books of Maccabees belong to the canon of Scripture. For Catholics, the Maccabean revolt was a "biblical" revolution in the strict sense. Yet there is no polemical intent in this description on my part. Even for those who do not accept 1—2 Maccabees as biblical books, the Maccabean revolt remains a biblical revolution in its goal to restore biblical religion and in its use of biblical events as prototypes and rallying-points. These books also serve the purpose of carrying on the story begun in the biblical book of Daniel.

Two other (noncanonical) books that bear the name "Maccabees" are not relevant to the topic of this book—the anatomy of the Maccabean revolution. Third Maccabees is set in the late third century B.C. and tells about the threat to Jewish life under Ptolemy IV Philopator, the king of Egypt (221-204 B.C.). Fourth Maccabees is a first-century A.D. philosophical discourse that takes as its starting point the martyrdoms of Eleazar and of the mother and her seven sons (see 2 Maccabees 6—7). Neither of these works can be considered as a primary source for studying the Maccabean revolt.

Historical Setting

The initial step in any historical investigation is the assembly of pertinent sources. The most important literary sources for the so-called Maccabean revolt are Daniel, 1 Maccabees, and 2 Maccabees. In comparison with other events in biblical times we have access to an abundance of historical sources for this event. But the quantity of sources is offset to some extent by the distinctive angles from which these sources tell their story. One simple way to summarize the specific tendencies of each work's approach to the Maccabean revolt is to attach the following headings: God's kingdom (Daniel), God's temple (2 Maccabees), and God's dynasty (1 Maccabees). Other sources (Testament of Moses, Judith, the Dead Sea scrolls, etc.) also deal in oblique ways with events that were part of the Maccabean revolt.

Before providing literary analyses of the sources, we must sketch the historical context in which the events described in them took place. In 538 B.C. with Cyrus the Great's capture of Babylon at least some Jews in Babylon were given permission to return to Jerusalem (see Isaiah 40-55). The restoration of Jerusalem and the Jewish community there was a slow and somewhat disappointing affair (see Haggai, Zechariah, Isaiah 56-66). But soon the Jewish community in Jerusalem was able to work out a liveable arrangement with their Persian rulers. Under Nehemiah and Ezra they achieved political stability and religious identity in the fifth century B.C. The conquest of the Persian empire by Alexander the Great brought a change of political masters to the land of Israel. At Alexander's death in 323 B.C. there was a good deal of political and military strife among his heirs, generals, and friends. By about 300 B.C. the succession had become clear—at least insofar as it concerned the people of Judea. They found themselves squeezed between two powerful dynasties: the Seleucids to the north and the Ptolemies to the south in Egypt. For the period between 300 and 200 Palestine was basically under the rule of the Ptolemies in Egypt. But in 200 B.C. Antiochus III had defeated the Ptolemies and brought the Jews of Palestine into his Seleucid empire. His successor, Seleucus IV (187-175 B.C.), was replaced eventually by Antiochus IV Epiphanes (175-163 B.C.). The accession of Antiochus IV marks the beginning of the story of the Maccabean revolt.

In the early years of Antiochus's reign the high priesthood exercised at the Jerusalem temple became a matter of controversy. The legitimate high priest Onias III was ousted in 175 B.C. by his brother Jason who promised Antiochus more revenue. In 172 B.C. Jason was outbid by Menelaus, who then served as high priest until 163 B.C. Eager to gain back the territories and power that Antiochus III had won and then lost, Antiochus IV invaded Egypt in 169 B.C. Always in need of more money, Antiochus IV returned by way of Jerusalem and plundered the temple there. His second campaign against Egypt (in 168) was not so successful, and he had to beat a hasty retreat. About the same time (168-165) several events took place in Jerusalem: The temple was plundered again, a fortress was established near the temple, the temple was desecrated, and a new form of worship was installed there.

These events form the background for the sources that we will now study. The most important dates are the following:

200: Palestine under Seleucid rule.
175: Antiochus IV seizes power.
168-165: Disturbing events occur in Jerusalem.

2

Daniel: God's Kingdom

The book of Daniel may appear at first sight to be a peculiar starting point for studying the Maccabean revolt. After all it records the exploits and visions of Daniel and his companions in the Babylonian and Persian courts. The narratives are set in the sixth and fifth centuries B.C., not the second century B.C. when the Maccabean revolt occurred. But the narrative setting of Daniel is not necessarily the setting in which the book was composed. In fact, the book of Daniel seems to have been put into its present Hebrew-Aramaic form precisely when the disturbing events described above were taking place in Jerusalem. There is no doubt that the book of Daniel contains some earlier traditions. Nevertheless, in its final form, it tells us more about the threat facing Israel in 168-165 B.C. than about the late Babylonian or early Persian periods. Thus Daniel is a major source for studying the Maccabean revolt.

From the perspective of literary forms, the book of Daniel falls into two parts: stories in which Daniel and his companions are described in the third person (chaps. 1-6), and visions in which Daniel narrates what had been revealed to him (chaps. 7-12). This neat literary division is complicated by the use of two languages. Chapters 1 and 8-12 are in Hebrew, and chapters 2-7 are in Aramaic.

The analysis that follows focuses on what these stories and visions may have meant to Jews around Jerusalem in 168-165 B.C. as they confronted the threat posed by Antiochus IV. At many levels the book of Daniel is complicated. But its basic message is simple: In the midst of the present trials, hold on!

God will soon bring in his kingdom, and Israel's enemies will be destroyed. The angle from which the book of Daniel approaches the events leading up to the Maccabean revolt is hope for God's kingdom.

Stories

The first chapter in the book of Daniel is set in the palace of the Babylonian king, Nebuchadnezzar, who was responsible for the capture and destruction of Jerusalem in the early sixth century B.C. Daniel and his three companions (Hananiah, Mishael, and Azariah) are being trained to serve in the royal palaces as scribes. During their three-year training period they were assigned "a daily portion of the rich food which the king ate, and of the wine which the king drank" (1:5). Daniel protested that sharing this food and drink would bring him into a state of ritual defilement (1:8). And so he proposes a ten-day test-period in which he and his companions will eat only vegetables and drink only water (1:12). At the end of ten days the four Jewish young men are found better in appearance and fatter than all the other youths who ate the king's rich food (1:15). Moreover, God gave to them learning and skill and to Daniel understanding in visions and dreams (1:17) so that they far surpassed their rivals.

How would this initial story of Daniel and his three companions at the Babylonian court have been understood by Palestinian Jews in the days of Antiochus IV? One of the issues facing the Jews of those days was observance of the traditional food laws, which had become a distinctive mark of Jewish identity. Antiochus sought to abrogate those laws, thus placing Jews in dilemma: Should they go along with this abrogation, or remain faithful to their customs? The answer coming from the book of Daniel is clear: Avoid the "defiling" food and drink offered by the king, and you will surely prosper. So a simple story set back in the sixth century B.C. sent forth a powerful message to Jews facing threats in the second century B.C. This same dynamic underlies all the stories in the first half of Daniel.

The remaining stories fall into two categories: contests

(chaps. 2, 4, 5) and conflicts (chaps. 3, 6). In the contests Daniel emerges as the wisest interpreter of dreams and visions. In the conflicts Daniel and his companions emerge unscathed from a dangerous situation because they trust in God and remain faithful to their religious principles. Both the contests and conflicts illumine the situation of the Jews in the second century and hold out a message of hope for the coming of God's kingdom.

The first contest (Daniel 2) involves King Nebuchadnezzar's dream and its interpretation. The king had a dream. He summons his wise men and challenges them to tell him both the dream and its interpretation (2:5). The interpreters are terrified by this challenge, and their only way out is to call on Daniel and his companions. After prayer, Daniel announces that he can tell the king his dream and its interpretation. His ability to do so is traced back to "the God in heaven who reveals mysteries" (2:28). At last Daniel provides the dream (2:31-35) and gives its interpretation (2:36-45). Then the king recognizes Daniel's God as "God of gods and Lord of kings, and a revealer of mysteries" (2:47).

Nebuchadnezzar's dream concerned the "idol with clay feet." Daniel's narrative of the dream proceeds as follows in Daniel 2:31-35:

> [31] "You saw, O King, and behold, a great image. This image, mighty and of exceeding brightness, stood before you, and its appearance was frightening. [32] The head of this image was of fine gold, its breast and arms of silver, its belly and thighs of bronze, [33] its legs of iron, its feet partly of iron and partly of clay. [34] As you looked, a stone was cut out by no human hand, and it smote the image on its feet of iron and clay, and broke them in pieces; [35] then the iron, the clay, the bronze, the silver, and the gold, all together were broken in pieces, and became like the chaff of the summer threshing floors; and the wind carried them away, so that not a trace of them could be found. But the stone that struck the image became a great mountain and filled the whole earth."

The interpretation given by Daniel in 2:36-45 relates the various parts of the statue to the great empires from Babylon in the sixth century to the Seleucids in the second century. King Nebuchadnezzar of Babylon is identified as the head of fine gold: "You are the head of gold" (2:38). The breast of fine silver and the belly and thighs of bronze are identified as the Medes and the Persians: "After you shall arise another kingdom inferior to you, and yet a third kingdom of bronze, which shall rule over all the earth" (2:39). The legs of iron are identified as the Greek kingdom of Alexander the Great "because iron breaks to pieces and shatters all things; and like iron which crushes, it shall break and crush all these" (2:40). The "feet partly of iron and partly of clay" refers to the "divided kingdom" (2:41) made up of the Seleucids and the Ptolemies. The interpretation alludes to unsuccessful attempts at alliance by means of marriages: "they will mix with one another in marriage, but they will not hold together, just as iron does not mix with clay" (2:43).

The dream describes the four great empires of the period from Israel's exile to the second century (Babylonian, Median, Persian, Greek) and the division of the Greek empire (Seleucids and Ptolemies). The climax of the dream comes when a stone "cut out by no human hand" (that is, by God's hand) strikes the feet, breaking them in pieces and causing the whole statue to disintegrate. Then "the God of heaven will set up a kingdom which shall never be destroyed, nor shall its sovereignty be left to another people" (2:44). To second-century B.C. Jews the message of the dream and its interpretation was clear: Try to look at history on the large scale. When you do so, then you can see the succession of empires and place the present threat in perspective. Trust that God will intervene soon and bring in his kingdom, which will mean peace and happiness for Israel.

The first conflict (Daniel 3) is occasioned by Nebuchadnezzar's decree that all persons "are to fall down and worship the golden image" that he set up on the plain of Dura, in the province of Babylon. Meanwhile, Daniel's three companions at the court—their Babylonian names are Shadrach, Meshach, and Abednego—had attained powerful positions in the province of Babylon (3:12). But the king's decree puts them in great danger: if they comply with it, they must abandon the worship of the true God; if they reject it, they will be cast into a burning fiery furnace (3:15). They reject the king's decree and place their fate in God's hand in the hope that God will rescue them. Though cast into the burning fiery furnace (3:20-23), they are preserved from harm by "one like a son of the gods" (3:25), who is most likely to be understood as an angel (3:28). In response to their miraculous rescue the king proclaims that no other god is able to deliver in this way and promotes the three Jews to even more prominent positions in the province of Babylon.

Whatever Antiochus IV intended to do with regard to worship at the Jerusalem temple, what was done there in 167 B.C. was perceived as the imposition of the cult of a foreign god. In such a situation the conflict story told in Daniel 3 sent forth a clear message: Remain faithful to the worship of Israel's God, and that God will surely rescue you from all harm. Thus a parallel is suggested between the Jewish heroes of old and Jews in the second century B.C.

The second contest (Daniel 4) involves another dream of Nebuchadnezzar and its interpretation. In this case the king narrates his dream to Daniel in Dan 4:10-17:

> [10]"The visions of my head as I lay in bed were these: I saw, and behold, a tree in the midst of the earth; and its height was great. [11]The tree grew and became strong, and its top reached to heaven, and it was visible to the end of the whole earth. [12]Its leaves were fair and its fruit abundant, and in it was food for all. The beasts of the field found shade under it, and the birds of the air dwelt in its branches, and all flesh was fed from it.
>
> [13]I saw in the visions of my head as I lay in bed, and behold, a watcher, a holy one, came down from heaven. [14]He cried aloud and said thus, 'Hew down the tree and cut off its branches, strip off its leaves and scatter its fruit; let the beasts flee from under it and the birds from its branches. [15]But leave the stump of its roots in the earth, bound with a band of iron and bronze, amid the tender grass of the field. Let him be wet with the dew of heaven; let his lot be with the beasts in the grass of the earth; [16]let his mind be changed from a man's, and let a beast's mind be given to him; and let seven times pass over him. [17]The sentence is by the decree of the watchers, the decision by the word of the holy ones, to

the end that the living may know that the Most High rules the kingdom of men, and gives it to whom he will, and sets over it the lowliest of men.'"

The unenviable task of interpreting the dream falls to Daniel: "The tree . . . it is you, O king" (4:20-22). The dream describes how the king will be driven out from among human beings and make his dwelling with the beasts of the field (4:25) so that the king may come to recognize that Heaven rules (4:26). A year later the dream becomes a reality when the king manifests his arrogance while walking on the roof of his palace in Babylon (4:28-33). At the end of the time appointed for his madness the king comes to recognize the King of heaven (4:34-37).

The "Prayer of Nabonidus," a brief work found among the Qumran scrolls, suggests that the story contained in Daniel 4 was earlier told about King Nabonidus, the successor of Nebuchadnezzar. Nabonidus was an enthusiastic promoter of the cult of the god Sin and spent ten years at the desert town of Teima in the Arabian peninsula. The priests of Marduk and others at Babylon resented these religious innovations and viewed Nabonidus as a crazy man and worse. Perhaps because of Nebuchadnezzar's involvement in the destruction of Jerusalem the story was transferred to him.

In the historical setting of the composition of the book of Daniel the story of the punishment of the crazy and arrogant king must have made readers think of Antiochus IV. The Greek title *epiphanēs* in his name means "(God) manifest." His opponents who knew well his arrogance and his erratic behavior played on the name, calling him *epimanēs* ("madman"). In the context of Antiochus IV Epiphanes's threats against the major institutions of Judaism, the message of Daniel 4 was clear: The king is a madman. But his arrogance and madness will be punished, and perhaps he will even come to recognize the God of Israel. In the meantime, wait, be faithful, and trust that God is at work.

The third contest (Daniel 5) is the episode of the "hand-writing on the wall." It takes place at a banquet hosted by the Babylonian king Belshazzar. The king orders that golden and silver vessels taken from the Jerusalem temple by Nebuchadnezzar be brought out and used. Despite Dan 5:2, Belshazzar was the son of Nabonidus, not of Nebuchadnezzar. As the guests at the banquet used the sacred vessels and praised their own gods, the fingers of a man's hand appeared and wrote on the plaster of the wall. No one could read the writing or give an interpretation. Finally Daniel is summoned to provide both the reading and the interpretation.

The reading is *"mene, mene, tekel,* and *parsin"* (7:25). The terms may have had some connection with sums of money— the mina, the shekel, and the half-shekel. Daniel's interpretation relates the words to the meaning of their Aramaic roots : *mnh* ("count, number"), *tkl* ("weigh"), and *prs* ("divide"). Each word refers to the end of the Babylonian empire: *mene* ("God has numbered the days of your kingdom and brought it to an end"); *tekel* ("you have been weighed in the balances and found wanting"); and *parsin* ("your kingdom is divided and given to the Medes and Persians").

The episode of the "handwriting on the wall" ostensibly concerns the end of the Babylonian empire in 538 B.C. at the hands of Cyrus the Great. But it also spoke to Jews in the second century B.C. Antiochus IV Epiphanes in his search for wealth to pay his armies and meet his expenses had plundered the Jerusalem temple and taken away from it some of the sacred vessels. The readers of Daniel surely drew the parallels between Belshazzar and Antiochus IV: The arrogant misuse of the temple vessels will soon be punished by God. The days of Antiochus IV have been counted out; he has been weighed and found wanting; and his kingdom will be taken away from him. The primary agent in bringing Antiochus IV to justice will be God. In the meantime wait and trust in God's power.

The second conflict (Daniel 6) follows the basic outline of the first (Daniel 3). Daniel is one of three presidents to whom other officials throughout the Median empire must give account. He soon becomes the most distinguished of all the officials (6:3), thus sparking off the jealousy of the others. Knowing that the only way to find fault with Daniel will be his practice of religion, the other officials convince King Darius to issue an irrevocable decree: "Whoever makes petition to any god or man for thirty days, except to you, O king, shall be cast into the den of lions" (6:7).

The royal decree has the effect of outlawing prayer. For

Daniel, the obligation to pray to the God of Israel outweighs the king's decree, and so "he got down on his knees three times a day and prayed and gave thanks before his God, as he had done previously" (6:10). His rivals knew that this would happen, and they report him to the king. Against his will and acting only because the royal decrees of the Medes and Persians are irrevocable, Darius condemns Daniel to be cast into the den of lions (6:16). He does so, however, with his own prayer: "May your God, whom you serve continually, deliver you!"

At dawn the next day Darius hurries to the den of lions and discovers Daniel to be alive and unharmed. Daniel explains: "My God sent his angel and shut the lions' mouths, and they have not hurt me" (6:22). Then Darius punishes Daniel's accusers in his place, restores Daniel to his position, and makes a decree about the power of the God of Daniel.

For second-century Jews under the threat of Antiochus IV the story of Daniel in the lions' den focused on the hero's fidelity to prayer to the God of Israel despite its terrible dangers. The suggestion is that, just as the God of Israel saved Daniel from all harm in the days of Darius, so too God will save those Jews who try to remain faithful in the days of Antiochus IV.

The contests and conflicts of the first half of the book of Daniel concern matters of great significance to second-century Jews: keeping the food laws, the end of Antiochus IV's kingdom, avoiding the worship of idols, dealing with a crazy king, the divine retribution for plundering the temple vessels, and fidelity to prayer. The Jewish heroes in these stories are wiser than all others, models of fidelity, and kept safe by God. The kings are alternately arrogant and sympathetic. But they remain under God's power.

Visions

The second half of the book of Daniel (chaps. 7-12) features visions narrated by Daniel in the first-person ("I"). There are three major visions: the Ancient of Days and the Son of Man (chap. 7), the Ram and the He-Goat (chap. 8), and the Outline of History from the Persian Period to the Death of Antiochus (chaps. 10-12). These visions are often described as "apocalypses." The word *apokalypsis* in Greek means "revelation." Here the visions reveal the course of Israel's history from the alleged time of Daniel the visionary to the time of the readers in the second century B.C. and beyond. As in the vision of the statue with clay feet in Daniel 2, there is a concern with charting out the empires and pointing to a time when God's kingdom will be made manifest. These visions encouraged second-century Jews to hold on to their practices and beliefs since they purported to reveal what the end of the Seleucid empire would be like and even hinted when it might happen.

The first and most famous of the visions is that of the Ancient of Days and the Son of Man in Daniel 7. It contains some enigmatic details and has exercised religious imaginations for more than two thousand years. But here our focus must be on the basic thrust of the text and its message for Jews in second-century B.C. Palestine.

The vision takes place in the first year of the Babylonian King Belshazzar (see Daniel 5). The vision begins with four great beasts coming out of the sea: the winged lion (7:4), the bear (7:5), the leopard (7:6), and the fourth beast (7:7-8). In light of the four-empire scheme in Daniel 2 and some hints in the text itself, it is possible to identify the winged lion with Babylon, the bear with the Medes, the leopard with the Persians, and the fourth beast with the Seleucids. The ten horns on the beast refer to the ten kings from Alexander the Great to Antiochus IV Epiphanes (at least according to one possible reckoning). The fourth beast's actions are described in negative ways: "devoured and broke in pieces and stamped..." (7:7).

The scene of the vision shifts suddenly to heaven for a judgment scene. The "one that was ancient of days" presides according to Dan 7:9-10. There is a mountain of scholarship on the details and background of this figure. For our purposes it is sufficient to say that the "one that was ancient of days" is the eternal one, the Most High God.

The vision continues in Dan 7:11-14:

¹¹I looked then because of the sound of the great words which the horn was speaking. And as I looked, the beast was slain, and its body destroyed and given over to be burned with fire. ¹²As for the rest of the beasts, their dominion was taken away, but their lives were prolonged for a season and a time. ¹³I saw in the night visions,
and behold, with the clouds of heaven
there came one like a son of man,
and he came to the Ancient of Days
and was presented before him.
¹⁴And to him was given dominion
and glory and kingdom,
that all peoples, nations, and languages
should serve him;
his dominion is an everlasting dominion,
which shall not pass away,
and his kingdom one
that shall not be destroyed.

The fourth beast is slain, and the power of the other enemies taken away (7:11-12). Then "one like a son of man" is presented before the throne. To him is given an eternal kingdom (7:13-14).

Who is the "one like a son of man?" Readers of the Gospels instinctively identify this figure as Jesus. But this is surely a later interpretation that the original audience of the book of Daniel could hardly have appreciated. One "*like* a son of man" suggests something or someone other than a human being. The most common interpretations today are the collective (Israel as a people) and the angelic (Michael as leader of the heavenly and earthly hosts). As we will see, both interpretations have a basis in the text of Daniel.

After a description of Daniel's reaction (7:15-16), there is a brief interpretation of the vision from an angelic interpreter: "These four great beasts are four kings who shall arise out of the earth. But the saints of the Most High shall receive the kingdom, and possess the kingdom for ever, for ever and ever" (7:17-18). The first part of the interpretation would seem to establish the identification of the four beasts with the four empires: Babylon, Media, Persia, and Greece. The second part would seem to indicate a connection between the "one like a son of man" and the "saints of the Most High," since both receive the eternal kingdom from God. This connection is evidence for the collective interpretation of the "one like a son of man."

Then after another description of Daniel's reaction and an elaboration of the fourth beast's war against the "saints of the Most High" (7:19-22), there is a lengthy interpretation of that struggle and its outcome in Dan 7:23-28 from the angelic interpreter:

> [23]"Thus he said: 'As for the fourth
> beast,
> there shall be a fourth kingdom on
> earth,
> which shall be different from all the
> kingdoms,
> and it shall devour the whole earth,
> and trample it down, and break it to pieces.
> [24]As for the ten horns,
> out of this kingdom
> ten kings shall arise,
> and another shall arise after them;
> he shall be different from the former
> ones,
> and shall put down three kings.
> [25]He shall speak words against the Most High,
> and shall wear out the saints of the
> Most High,
> and shall think to change the times
> and the law;
> and they shall be given into his hand
> for a time, two times, and half a time.
> [26]But the court shall sit in judgment, and his dominion shall
> be taken
> away,
> to be consumed and destroyed to the end.
> [27]And the kingdom and the dominion
> and the greatness of the kingdoms
> under the whole heaven

> shall be given to the people of the
> saints of the Most High;
> their kingdom shall be an everlasting
> kingdom ,
> and all dominions shall serve and obey them.'
> [28]"Here is the end of the matter. As for me, Daniel, my
> thoughts greatly alarmed me, and my color changed; but I
> kept the matter in my mind."

By now most of this material is familiar. There are, however, two new features. The "saints of the Most High" to whom the kingdom is given (7:27) are also the object of Antiochus's stratagem (7:25), another indication of the collective interpretation of the "one like a son of man" as Israel. The second new feature is the appearance of a timetable for Antiochus's domination over Israel: "they shall be given into his hand for a time, two times, and a half a time" (7:25). What precisely this forecast meant is difficult to know. But it is the first of several timetables in the second half of the book of Daniel.

For all its fascinating details and problems of interpretation the vision of the Ancient Days and the Son of Man is quite clear in its basic message: The domination of Antiochus IV will end soon; then the kingdom will be handed over to the saints of the Most High (which is either the collective Israel or at least includes Israel).

The vision of the Ram and the He-Goat (Dan 8:1-14) receives an interpretation (8:15-26) that helps us to understand it in terms of the world empires familiar to us from chapters 2 and 7. The ram charging in all directions (8:3-4) represents the kings of Media and Persia (8:20). The he-goat charging from the west and trampling the ram (8:5-8) is the king of Greece (8:21), Alexander the Great. The four horns arising from the great horn (8:8) are the four kingdoms into which Alexander's empire was divided (8:22).

The "little horn" (8:9) is Antiochus IV. Among the arrogant deeds attributed to him the one that was especially outrageous to second-century Jews was Antiochus IV's causing the daily sacrifice (or "continual burnt offering") to cease and overthrowing the sanctuary. There is also the charge that he set up "the transgression that makes desolate" (or the "abomination of desolation," as it is often called). An angelic figure warns that this terrible state of affairs has a time-limit of 2,300 evenings and mornings—a little more than three years (8:14). Then the sanctuary shall be restored to its rightful state. His defeat will be accomplished "by no human hand" (8:25), therefore by God's own hand or that of his angelic hosts. The message is basically the same as that of the preceding vision: The domination of Antiochus IV will end soon. Then things will be made right again.

The lament in Daniel 9 is a kind of interlude or change of pace. It is important first of all because it explains why these terrible events have befallen the Jews of Jerusalem and environs: "We have sinned and done wrong and acted wickedly and rebelled ... we have sinned, we have done wickedly" (9:5, 15). Daniel's prayer is that God let his anger and wrath turn away from Jerusalem (9:16). Up to this point in the book of Daniel there had been no reflection on why these terrible things happened and why the fiendish Antiochus IV had been unleashed against Jerusalem. Here we get the traditional prophetic explanation that Antiochus IV's activities at Jerusalem were a punishment for the sins of the people.

Another reason for the importance of chapter 9 is its contribution to the timetable of events. At the very beginning of the lament (9:2) Daniel alludes to Jeremiah's prophecy that Israel would be in exile and Jerusalem in ruins for seventy years (see Jer 25:11-12; 29:10). At the end (9:24-27) Daniel talks about seventy weeks of years, which equals 490 years:

> [24]"Seventy weeks of years are decreed concerning your people and your holy city, to finish the transgression, to put an end to sin, and to atone for iniquity, to bring in everlasting righteousness, to seal both vision and prophet, and to anoint a most holy place. [25]Know therefore and understand that from the going forth of the word to restore and build Jerusalem to the coming of an anointed one, a prince, there shall be seven weeks. Then for sixty-two weeks it shall be built again with squares and moat, but in a troubled time. [26]And after the sixty-two weeks, an anointed one shall be cut off, and shall have nothing; and the people of the prince who is to come shall destroy the city and the

sanctuary. Its end shall come with a flood, and to the end there shall be war: desolations are decreed. ²⁷And he shall make a strong covenant with many for one week; and for half of the week he shall cause sacrifice and offering to cease; and upon the wing of abominations shall come one who makes desolate, until the decreed end is poured out on the desolator."

The "anointed one" who shall be cut off (9:26) must be the legitimate high priest Onias III. The major figure in the final week is the prince, surely Antiochus IV. What is new here is the hint that he had support among Jews in Jerusalem: "And he shall make a strong covenant with many for one week" (9:27). So chapter 9 explains Antiochus IV's actions as punishment for Israel's sins and gives another timetable indicating the closeness of the end.

The core of the third and final vision (Daniel 10-12) is the historical survey in Dan 11:2-12:4. It is introduced by the account of Daniel's encounter with the angelic figure (10:1-21), and concluded by more timetables (12:5-13). The third vision provides important information about relations between the Seleucids and the Ptolemies and ends with a picture of the future kingdom of God. Its basic message to second-century Jews was the familiar message of the other dreams and visions about world history: God is in control; the time allotted to Israel's enemies is short; God's kingdom will come soon.

After summarizing the Persian period (11:2) and describing Alexander the Great and the breakup of his empire (11:3-4), Daniel describes the early Seleucids and Ptolemies in 11:5-20: Ptolemy I Soter (323-285 B.C.) and Seleucus I Nicator (312/311-280) in 11:5, the failed marriage alliance between Ptolemy II Philadelphus (285-246) and Antiochus II Theos (261-246) in 11:6, the revenge taken by Ptolemy III Euergetes (246-221) for the death of his sister Berenice by overrunning the kingdom of Seleucus II Callinicus (246-226) in 11:7-9, and the reign of Antiochus III (223-187) in 11:10-19—the campaign (219-217) against Ptolemy IV Philopator in 11:10-12, the joint campaign with Philip V of Macedon in 199 against Ptolemy V Epiphanes (203-181) in 11:13-14, the siege and capture of Sidon and Palestine (198) in 11:15-16, his peace treaty with

Ptolemy V and abortive marriage alliance in 11:17, his attacks on coastal towns and defeat by the Roman Scipio at Thermopylae (191) in 11:18, and his death while plundering the sanctuary of Bel (187) in 11:19. The reign of his successor, Seleucus IV Philopator (187-175), who was the brother of Antiochus IV, is summarized in a single verse (11:20): He sent out a tribute-collector and died without glory.

Now the stage is set for the description of Antiochus IV Epiphanes (175-164 B.C.) in Dan 11:21-45. This description was apparently written before Antiochus's death, since the part about his death (11:40-45) contradicts what is known from other sources. But up to that point the vision is a fairly accurate (though sometimes mysterious) presentation of Antiochus's career.

After introducing Antiochus as a "contemptible person" and alluding to his devious method of obtaining the Seleucid throne (11:21), Daniel foresees his consolidation of power and deposing the legitimate Jewish high priest Onias III (11:22-24). Then he describes Antiochus's first campaign against Egypt (11:25-28) and his second campaign (11:29-30). There are allusions in Dan 11:28 and 30 to Antiochus's plundering the sacred vessels and other wealth of the Jerusalem temple. There is also notice in 11:30 that his second Egyptian campaign was cut short by intervention of the Romans: "For the ships of the Kittim shall come against him, and he shall be afraid and withdraw." The term "Kittim," which originally referred to people of Cyprus, was used in this time to describe the Romans.

Humiliated by the Romans, Antiochus IV turned to Jerusalem according to Dan 11:30-35:

> [30]For ships of Kittim shall come against him, and he shall be afraid and withdraw, and shall turn back and be enraged and take action against the holy covenant. He shall turn back and give heed to those who forsake the holy covenant. [31]Forces from him shall appear and profane the temple and fortress, and shall take away the continual burnt offering. And they shall set up the abomination that makes desolate. [32]He shall seduce with flattery those who violate the covenant; but the people who know their God shall stand

firm and take action. [33]And those among the people who are wise shall make many understand, though they shall fall by sword and flame, by captivity and plunder, for some days. [34]When they fall, they shall receive a little help. And many shall join themselves to them with flattery. [35]And some of those who are wise shall fall, to refine and to cleanse them and to make them white, until the time of the end, for it is yet for the time appointed.

The text contains some features that will be made clearer as we proceed in our survey of sources. At this stage we need only point them out. First, Antiochus IV appears to have some support among Jews in Jerusalem: "He shall turn back and give heed to those who forsake the holy covenant" (11:30); "He shall seduce with flattery those who violate the covenant" (11:32). Second, the text describes what Antiochus did to the temple: He profaned it (11:31), took away the daily sacrifice there (11:31), and set up the "abomination that makes desolate" (11:31). But he is also said to have profaned the fortress (11:31), presumably an allusion to Antiochus's establishing in the fortress near the temple a garrison of troops loyal to him. This garrison will prove remarkably long-lived, as 1 Maccabees indicates.

A third important feature in the text is its acknowledgment of various groups within Israel. Mention has already been made of the Jewish allies/supporters of Antiochus IV (11:30, 32). A second group is constituted by the "wise" (11:33) who stand firm and try to make others understand. There are allusions to painful sufferings among the wise: "though they shall fall by sword and flame, by captivity and plunder, for some days" (11:33). There are also indications of defections ("some of those who are wise shall fall," 11:35) and widespread popularity ("many shall join themselves to them with flattery," 11:34). When describing the sufferings of the wise (11:34), the text says that "they shall receive a little help." Some interpreters find in this a rather slighting reference to the early Maccabean movement. At any rate, the author of the book was really concerned with the "wise." He surely belonged to this circle and wrote to encourage other members to hold firm "until the time of the end" (11:35). Unlike the Maccabees, his approach is nonviolent, leaving it to God to end the attacks against Israel and to bring in the kingdom.

This description of Antiochus's activities in Jerusalem and Jewish responses to them is followed by a vigorous denunciation of his arrogance (11:36-39). Then there is a prediction of Antiochus's death in 11:40-45, which supposes that after glorious conquests he would meet his death in the land of Israel ("he shall pitch his palatial tents between the sea and the glorious holy mountain," 11:45). Various accounts of Antiochus's death are analyzed and compared on pages 97-103. Here it is sufficient to note that Antiochus died in Persia and did not do all the things attributed to him in Dan 11:40-45. These facts suggest that the author wrote before the death of Antiochus IV and that Dan 11:40-45 is more prediction than are the early sections of chapter 11. This negative conclusion allows a positive one: A representative of the "wise" composed the book of Daniel after Antiochus's attacks had begun but before Jewish resistance was galvanized to retake the Jerusalem temple in 164 B.C.

The historical survey outlined in Daniel 11 reaches a climax in Dan 12:1-3:

> [1]At that time shall arise Michael, the great prince who has charge of your people. And there shall be a time of trouble, such as never has been since there was a nation till that time; but at that time your people shall be delivered, every one whose name shall be found written in the book. [2]And many of those who sleep in the dust of the earth shall awake, some to everlasting life, and some to shame and everlasting contempt. [3]And those who are wise shall shine like the brightness of the firmament; and those who turn many to righteousness, like the stars for ever and ever.

The theological significance of this text for belief in the resurrection of the dead should be obvious. Here we are interested only in its significance for the crisis facing second-century Palestinian Jews. The text envisions a great battle in which the archangel Michael will fight on behalf of the people of God. Statements like these lead some interpreters to identify the "one like a son of man" in Dan 7:13-14 as Michael, despite the collective interpretations given in later parts of chapter 7. The resurrection of the dead takes place after Michael's victory and the deliverance of God's people. At the resurrection the dead will be divided into two groups: those who awake to everlasting life, and those who awake to shame and everlasting contempt (12:2). The "wise" will receive a special reward; they will shine like the stars (12:3). The nagging questions "how long shall it be?" (12:6) receives an answer from the angelic interpreter: "a time, two times, and half a time" (12:7; see 7:25). This enigmatic response then receives two specifications. The first (12:11) counts 1,290 days (about three and a half years) from Antiochus's suspension of the daily sacrifice in 167 B.C. The second figure (12:12) lengthens the time to 1,334 days. These figures have generated many interpretations and much controversy through the centuries. For our purposes what is significant is the sequence of events: Antiochus had desecrated the temple in 167 B.C. The author of Daniel wrote about 165 B.C. and expected that Antiochus would die in defeat and the kingdom would be handed over to the saints of the Most High in 164 or 163 B.C.

Historical Value

At the beginning of this analysis, the book of Daniel was described as a major source for studying the Maccabean revolt. Through the contests and conflicts of the first half and through the three major visions of the second half, one basic message is developed: In the midst of the present trials, hold on! God will soon bring in his kingdom, and Israel's enemies will be destroyed. The book of Daniel represents the position of the "wise" who look to God to get his people out of their present troubles. There is a pathetic element to the text's certainties about the when and how of a deliverance that never came. The book was written in the middle of the crisis.

The value of the book of Daniel as a historical source of the Maccabean revolt is offset to some extent by the literary character of the work. The book communicates through a code according to which characters and events set back in the Babylonian and Persian periods parallel characters and events in the second century B.C. Whether for reasons of political safety or a desire to create an esoteric atmosphere, the work seldom communicates directly, using real names and real places. Thus the interpreter is challenged to solve the puzzles set forth by the text. The circle to which the author belonged ("the wise") remains shadowy until near the end of the book. The author supplies some information about the nature of the crisis precipitated by Antiochus IV and refers to some actions that he took. But this information is sketchy and allusive at best, and mysterious at worst. He gives an explanation for why these events befell the Jews of Jerusalem—as punishment for their sins. Yet this theological explanation is vague and shopworn. Of course, we should not blame a second-century B.C. writer for failing to write a modern historical account. And we should be grateful for the "eyewitness" character of his work and the fascinating ways in which he presented his message. But if we want to know more about the nature of the crisis in second-century B.C. Palestine and about its leading characters, we must turn to 2 Maccabees.

3

Second Maccabees: God's Temple

In comparison with the allusive and often mysterious book of Daniel, 2 Maccabees seems to be promising source for studying the Maccabean revolt. Written after the initial successes of Judas Maccabeus and his companions and from the relative security of the resolution of the crisis facing the Jews of Palestine in the second century B.C., 2 Maccabees names persons and places directly and abundantly. It enables us to fill out some of the enigmatic details mentioned in the book of Daniel and to follow the story down to 161 B.C. But its obvious value as a historical source is tempered to some extent by its complicated history of composition and its narrow focus on the safety of the Jerusalem temple. One interpreter has even described 2 Maccabees as "temple propaganda." Whatever merits that description might have, it does express the peculiar angle from which 2 Maccabees views the Maccabean revolt. Whereas the book of Daniel emphasizes God's kingdom, 2 Maccabees emphasizes God's temple.

The best point of entry into the complicated composition history of 2 Maccabees is the author's own statement in 2 Macc 2:19-32. There he summarizes the subject matter of the book in 2:19-22: the exploits of Judas and his brothers against Antiochus IV and his son Antiochus V, and how with God's help these few men were able to recover the temple, free the city, and restore the laws. Then in 2:23 he identifies his own work as a digest of a longer work by Jason of Cyrene: "All this which has been set forth by Jason of Cyrene in five volumes, we shall attempt to condense into a single book." He goes on in

2:24-32 to describe his work as a condenser in an engaging way, comparing himself to a decorator at work on a house that has already been built. He wants to entertain his readers ("to please those who wish to read," 2:25) and does not pretend to give an exhaustive treatment (2:31).

The forthright and engaging way in which the author of 2 Maccabees expresses himself in his preface (2:19-32) can mask several critical problems involved in using 2 Maccabees as a historical source. The first and most obvious problem concerns the relationship between the original five-volume work of Jason of Cyrene and the one-volume work known now as 2 Maccabees. The original language of both works appears to have been Greek. But there is no way of knowing how closely the epitomator (as he is often called) followed the style and vocabulary of Jason of Cyrene. Furthermore, there is no way of knowing what the epitomator left out from or added into Jason's story in his attempt to be entertaining and to tell the tale from his own perspective.

The story ends in 161 B.C. with the defeat of Nicanor and before the death of Judas Maccabeus. The rather abrupt conclusion and the absence of any indication of Judas's death suggest that Jason wrote just about the time at which he ended the story. At least, such a hypothesis is plausible. But when did the epitomator do his work? Was it shortly after the original composition, or was it in the late-second or even early-first century B.C.?

In this survey of historical sources regarding the Maccabean revolt, I am treating 2 Maccabees before 1 Maccabees primarily for pedagogical reasons, not because I have firm opinions about their order of composition. 2 Maccabees continues the story begun in the book of Daniel and takes it down to 161 B.C. It supplies important data concerning the persons and events of the Maccabean revolt. 1 Maccabees takes the story down to the late second century B.C. This order of presentation makes the sequence of events easier to understand. But it may not reflect the order in which these books were composed.

The distinctive angle from which the author of 2 Maccabees (that is, the epitomator of Jason's five-volume work) viewed the events that he described involved the fate of the Jerusalem temple. Two letters are prefixed to the author's preface (2:19-32). The first letter (1:1-9) is from Jews in Jerusalem to Jews in Egypt in which the former encourage the latter to celebrate the feast of the Dedication of the Temple (now usually called Hanukkah)—the rededication of the Jerusalem temple by Judas and his companions in late 164 B.C. The first letter is dated in the one hundred and eighty-eighth year. Since this dating system counts from 312/311 B.C. as the first year of the Seleucid era, its equivalent in our system would be 124 B.C. It is possible that the epitome of Jason's work was sent along with this letter from Jerusalem to Egypt. In fact, the epitome may even have been prepared for this specific occasion.

The second letter (1:10-2:18) is undated. It is from Jews in Jerusalem to a prominent Egyptian Jew named Aristobulus and the other Jews in Egypt. It too seeks to explain why Egyptian Jews should celebrate Hanukkah and traces the "feast of fire" back to the days of Nehemiah (1:18).

While extraneous to the main story in 2 Maccabees, the prefixed letters (1:1-9; 1:10-2:18) indicate that the celebration of Hanukkah by Jews outside the land of Israel was controversial. The Egyptian Jews clearly needed to be convinced on this matter. Part of their resistance may have stemmed from the fact that the first Hanukkah took place in Jerusalem in 164 B.C. The Jews of Egypt may have looked upon this feast as a parochial concern. Or they may have thought that events should have gone in another direction than that of the emergence of a Maccabean dynasty. Still another objection may have been the recent character of the events being celebrated. Only forty years had passed between the first Hanukkah (164 B.C.) and the first letter (124 B.C.). The feast was not ancient and had no foundation in the Hebrew Bible.

Between the epitomator's preface (2:19-32) and his conclusion (15:37-39), the main part of 2 Maccabees narrates three attacks on the Jerusalem temple and the successful defense of the temple by God and the people of Israel. The first attack took place under Seleucus IV when Heliodorus tried to plunder the temple treasury (3:1-40). The second attack occurred under Antiochus IV Epiphanes and issued in the capture of the temple and its rededication by Judas (4:1-10:9). The third attack happened under Antiochus V and involved the defeat of his general Nicanor as he tried to kill Judas Maccabeus (10:10-15:36). This outline of the three attacks on the Jerusalem temple does not account for everything presented in 2 Maccabees 3-15. But it does highlight what clearly were the major events for the author.

Heliodorus

Heliodorus's attempt at despoiling the temple treasury (3:1-40) is really an overture to or preview of the other two attacks on the Jerusalem temple. The main character is Heliodorus, who was sent by Seleucus IV (187-175 B.C.) to confiscate the wealth stored at the temple treasury. The mission of Heliodorus was prompted by events within the Jewish community at Jerusalem. The author describes the Jewish high priest Onias III as an exemplary leader—so successful that Seleucus even contributed to the upkeep of the temple and its services (3:1-3). But a certain Simon had a disagreement with Onias III "about the administration of the city market" (3:4). Failing to get his way, Simon went to the governor Apollonius with the report that the temple treasury in Jerusalem contained enormous amounts of wealth and that Seleucus could get control over it. Apollonius told the king, who sent Heliodorus to check out the report.

The stage is set for the first attack on the temple. Even though the high priest Onias III tries to explain that there really is not much wealth at all in the temple treasury, he cannot dissuade Heliodorus from carrying out his mission (3:13-14). The prospect of his profaning the temple sends the people into a panic (3:15-21), and they beg God to intervene against Heliodorus. Just as Heliodorus and his companions arrive at the temple treasury, they are driven off by a fearsome rider and two young men who defend the temple and thrash Heliodorus to the point of death (3:22-30). Only through the mediation of the high priest Onias III is Heliodorus rescued from death and restored to health. Heliodorus sends back to Seleucus IV the lesson that he has learned from the incident: "If you have any enemy or plotter against your government, send him there, for you will get him back thoroughly scourged, if he escapes at all, for there certainly is about the place some power of God" (3:38).

In several respects the Heliodorus episode is an overture to what follows and so alerts us to what we should expect in the other episodes. There are tensions within the Jewish community in Jerusalem; in this case between Onias III and Simon. One side, Simon's, tries to resolve the tensions by appealing to the Seleucids, who thus involve themselves in Jewish affairs. The result of the Seleucid intervention is the threat that the Jerusalem temple will be profaned. The attempt at profaning the temple fails only because God intervenes to protect the temple and his people.

The chief difference between the Heliodorus episode and those that follow it concerns the nature of God's intervention. It would be fair to call the divine intervention in the Heliodorus episode "miraculous" or "supernatural." The rider and the two young men appear out of nowhere, do their job, and disappear. They seem angelic, not human. In the remaining two threats God intervenes through the efforts of human beings—through Judas Maccabeus and his companions.

Antiochus IV Epiphanes

Even after the Heliodorus incident the intrigues surrounding the high priesthood in Jerusalem continued (4:1-6). Simon now claimed that Heliodorus had been incited by Onias III to try to seize the temple treasury. We are to presume that Heliodorus and Onias III were now friends, and this slander was Simon's way of revenge and keeping his own interests alive. Simon also gained the governor Apollonius as an ally and even resorted to murder (4:3). Onias sought to warn Seleucus IV about his true enemies and their plots but was prevented by the death of Seleucus IV and the eventual succession of his brother, Antiochus IV Epiphanes.

At this point (175 B.C.) the high priesthood passed from Onias III to Jason, his brother, because Jason promised Antiochus IV 360 talents of silver plus 80 talents more from another source of revenue. It was not unusual that the Seleucid king should have final approval over the office of the Jewish high priesthood. Nor was it unusual that Antiochus IV was in desperate need of money and thus willing to accommodate the desires of Jason. Nor would all Jews be outraged at the transition, since Jason (whose Hebrew name was probably Joshua) at least belonged to the legitimate high-priestly family. To clinch his agreement with Antiochus IV, Jason went further in his offer and outlined a whole program for the Jewish people in Jerusalem in 2 Macc 4:9-17:

> [9]In addition to this he promised to pay one hundred and fifty more if permission were given to establish by his authority a gymnasium and a body of youth for it, and to enrol the men of Jerusalem as citizens of Antioch. [10]When the king assented and Jason came to office, he at once shifted his countrymen over to the Greek way of life. [11]He set aside the existing royal concessions to the Jews, secured through John the father of Eupolemus, who went on the mission to establish friendship and alliance with the Romans; and he destroyed the lawful ways of living and introduced new customs contrary to the law. [12]For with alacrity he founded a gymnasium right under the citadel, and he induced the noblest of the young men to wear the Greek hat. [13]There was such an extreme of Hellenization and increase in the adoption of foreign ways because of the surpassing wickedness of Jason, who was ungodly and no high priest, [14]that the priests were no longer intent upon their service at the altar. Despising the sanctuary and neglecting the sacrifices, they hastened to take part in the unlawful proceedings in the wrestling arena after the call to the discus, [15]disdaining the honors prized by their fathers and putting the highest value upon Greek forms of prestige. [16]For this reason heavy disaster overtook them, and those whose ways of living they admired and wished to imitate completely became their enemies and punished them. [17]For it is no light thing to show irreverence to the divine laws—a fact which later events will make clear.

The author of 2 Maccabees presents Jason's program as a wholesale shift over to the Greek way of life. How radical this shift appeared to Jerusalem Jews already accustomed to Greek ways in some areas remains a matter of debate. But the author of 2 Maccabees was clearly horrified by what he interpreted as a very radical move on Jason's part.

The shift included the promotion of Greek institutions: the gymnasium (the institution for bodily exercise and imparting Greek culture), the ephebate (the body of youth enrolled in the gymnasium), and enrolling men of Jerusalem as (honorary) citizens of Antioch. The references to Jason's setting aside the existing royal concessions (4:11) and destroying the lawful ways of living to introduce new customs contrary to the law (4:11) describe the replacement of the Torah as the official law in Israel. The placement of the gymnasium right under the citadel near the temple and the inducing the young men to wear the wide-brim Greek (or "Hermes") hat (4:12) are traced to "the surpassing wickedness of Jason, who was ungodly and no high priest" (4:13). So great is the impact of this program of Hellenization that the priests serving at the temple show more interest in going to the wrestling matches than in caring for the sanctuary and carrying out the sacrifices (4:14-15)! To Jason's program of Hellenization the evils about to befall Israel are traced (4:16-17); they are punishments for the sins of at least some of the people of Israel (see Daniel 9).

The ambiguities involved in joining Judaism and Hellenism are brought out by the incident involving the quadrennial games at Tyre (4:18-20). Jason sent envoys with three-hundred silver drachmas for the sacrifice to Hercules. But the envoys apparently developed scruples and applied it to the construction of ships. According to 4:22 Antiochus was accorded a gracious welcome to Jerusalem by the high priest Jason and the citizens in 172 B.C.

If the author of 2 Maccabees was outraged at the high priesthood of Jason, how much more was he angered at the accession to that office in 172 B.C. by Simon's brother, Menelaus (4:23-29)! Menelaus obtained the office through outbidding Jason by three-hundred talents, thus visiting on Jason an appropriate reward for his own arrogance. Even worse in character than Jason was, he had absolutely no qualification for the office of Jewish high priest. At least Jason had belonged to a priestly family. Menelaus could not even claim that distinction, for he was from the tribe of Benjamin (see 2 Macc 3:4).

Menelaus is described as "the chief plotter against his fellow citizens" (4:50). Much of chapter 4 involves the reasons for such a description. When Menelaus was called on the carpet by Antiochus to explain why he failed to make good on his promised payments and the king was distracted by revolts in Tarsus and Mallus (4:30), Menelaus hit upon the strategy of confiscating the temple vessels to pay his debts and to raise money by selling them (4:32). When Onias III began to expose Menelaus's strategy, Menelaus plotted with the Seleucid deputy Andronicus to have Onias killed. Even Antiochus was outraged at this plot and had Andronicus punished and killed.

Menelaus's strategy of temple robbing also raised opposition in Jerusalem: "the populace gathered against Lysimachus [Menelaus's brother] because many of the gold vessels had already been stolen" (4:39). Lysimachus himself was killed in a popular uprising: "the temple robber himself they killed close by the treasury" (4:42). Then at Tyre the Jewish opposition was allowed to plead its case against Menelaus before Antiochus IV (4:44). Knowing that he was going to be convicted, Menelaus bribed Ptolemy to win the king over to his side. The result was that Menelaus was freed and his Jewish accusers put to death (4:47). The author notes that even the Tyrians recognized the enormity of this travesty of justice (4:49).

During Antiochus's invasion of Egypt (169 B.C.) there was an atmosphere of ferment in Jerusalem (5:1-4). When the false rumor arose that Antiochus had died in Egypt, Jason tried to regain the high priesthood by assaulting the city. In the end Menelaus held onto power, and Jason had to flee. The author seems to take pleasure in narrating Jason's miserable end in 5:7-10:

> [7]He did not gain control of the government, however; and in the end got only disgrace from his conspiracy, and fled again into the country of the Ammonites. [8]Finally he met a miserable end. Accused before Aretas the ruler of the Arabs, fleeing from city to city, pursued by all men, hated as a rebel against the laws, and abhorred as the executioner of his country and his fellow citizens, he was cast ashore in Egypt; [9]and he who had driven many from their own

country into exile died in exile, having embarked to go to the Lacedaemonians in hope of finding protection because of their kinship. [10]He who had cast out many to lie unburied had no one to mourn for him; he had no funeral of any sort and no place in the tomb of his fathers.

Assuming that all Judea was in revolt and smarting from being forced out of Egypt by the Romans (see Dan 11:30), Antiochus put down the insurrection with brutality, supposedly being responsible for the death of 80,000 in three days and selling as many into slavery. His arrival in Jerusalem and triumph there lead the high priest Menelaus to give him a tour of the temple and provide the occasion for him to appropriate the sacred vessels (5:15-16). What galls the author most of all is that Menelaus served as Antiochus's guide in this foray. This intolerable situation in turn leads the author to reflect on why these events were happening in Israel:

> [15]Not content with this, Antiochus dared to enter the most holy temple in all the world, guided by Menelaus, who had become a traitor both to the laws and to his country. [16]He took the holy vessels with his polluted hands, and swept away with profane hands the votive offerings which other kings had made to enhance the glory and honor of the place. [17]Antiochus was elated in spirit, and did not perceive that the Lord was angered for a little while because of the sins of those who dwelt in the city, and that therefore he was disregarding the holy place. [18]But if it had not happened that they were involved in many sins, this man would have been scourged and turned back from his rash act as soon as he came forward, just as Heliodorus was, whom Seleucus the king sent to inspect the treasury. [19]But the Lord did not choose the nation for the sake of the holy place, but the place for the sake of the nation. [20]Therefore the place itself shared in the misfortunes that befell the nation and afterward participated in its benefits; and what was forsaken in the wrath of the Almighty was restored again in all its glory when the great Lord became reconciled.

These events happened because of the people's sins (see 4:16-17). Because of their many sins, God did not intervene in the miraculous or spectacular way that he did in the Heliodorus incident. Because of the close relationship between the people and the Jerusalem temple, God allowed the temple to be profaned on account of the people's sins. Yet even in this dark moment in history, the author holds out the prospect of a bright future for both people and temple "when the great Lord became reconciled" (5:20). Thus the author states his basic theology of the events befalling Israel in those days.

In the aftermath of Antiochus's plundering the Jerusalem temple with Menelaus as his guide there was even greater pressure (5:21-26) on the Jews of Jerusalem and environs: Menelaus was still high priest, barbarous governors were appointed at Jerusalem and Gerizim, and Apollonius was sent to attack Jerusalem on the Sabbath. But again a note of hope is sounded, this time with the first reference to Judas Maccabeus in 5:27:

> [27]But Judas Maccabeus, with about nine others, got away to the wilderness, and kept himself and his companions alive in the mountains as wild animals do; they continued to live on what grew wild, so that they might not share in the defilement.

Note that there is no mention here of Judas's father and brothers (as in 1 Maccabees). The author of 2 Maccabees shows no interest in the Maccabean family or dynasty. The interest in Judas lies mainly in his exploits as God's instrument in defending and restoring the Jerusalem temple.

Meanwhile back in Jerusalem the profanation of the temple reaches a new level according to 6:1-6:

> [1]Not long after this, the king sent an Athenian senator to compel the Jews to forsake the laws of their fathers and cease to live by the laws of God, [2]and also to pollute the temple in Jerusalem and call it the temple of Olympian Zeus, and to call the one in Gerizim the temple of Zeus the Friend of Strangers, as did the people who dwelt in that place.

³Harsh and utterly grievous was the onslaught of evil. ⁴For the temple was filled with debauchery and reveling by the Gentiles, who dallied with harlots and had intercourse with women within the sacred precincts, and besides brought in things for sacrifice that were unfit. ⁵The altar was covered with abominable offerings which were forbidden by the laws. ⁶A man could neither keep the sabbath, nor observe the feasts of his fathers, nor so much as confess himself to be a Jew.

Commentators often point to a concentric or chiastic structure in this text, with 6:3 ("Harsh and utterly grievous was the onslaught of evil") as the center. The beginning (6:1) and end (6:6) of the text deal with the compulsion to abandon the Jewish laws; between the extremes and the center there are references to the profanation of the temple (6:2, 4-5).

What 2 Macc 6:1-6 describes here is what the book of Daniel referred to as the "abomination of desolation." The first description (6:2) suggests the transformation of the Jerusalem temple into a shrine to the Greek Olympian Zeus and the Gerizim temple into a shrine to the Greek Zeus Xenios ("friend of strangers"). It would be wise not to lay too much emphasis on the *Greek* dimension of the new cults; the names seem to be basically translations according to the practice of *interpretatio Graeca* of essential themes already connected with the cult places at Jerusalem and Gerizim. The allegation of cultic prostitution made in 6:4 also does not fit Greek religion.

If the cults introduced at Jerusalem and Gerizim were not Greek, what were they? The question will be addressed in chapter five, though no answer to it is totally satisfying. The author of 2 Maccabees, however, presents the new cults as part of a campaign to force Jews "to change over to Greek customs" (6:9). He reports that Jews were forced to celebrate the king's birthday every month and to walk in processions honoring Dionysus, the god of wine and the grape harvest (6:7).

The misery that came upon the Jewish people reaches its climax in stories of the martyrs (6:10-7:42). Here we are interested first in why these martyrs are said to die. First (6:10) two women are tormented and killed for having circumcised their children. Then (6:11) others are burned while hiding in nearby caves in order to observe the Sabbath. Next Eleazar the scribe (6:18-31) refuses to eat pork; he refuses even to feign doing so, lest it be thought that he went over to an "alien religion" in his old age. The final and most famous incident (7:1-42) involves the woman and her seven sons who are tortured and executed for refusing "to partake of unlawful swine's flesh" (7:2). So the grounds for martyrdom are some of the practices that made Jews distinctive in the Greco-Roman world: circumcision, Sabbath observance, and food laws.

Chapter seven is probably the best known part of 2 Maccabees. It tells the story of the martyrdoms of the mother and her seven sons. Each of the seven sons is brought forward before the king, is tortured, and explains why he is going through the suffering. At two points (7:20-23, 26-29) the mother intervenes. She dies last of all, after her sons (7:41).

Besides giving the grounds for which the martyrs underwent death, the text also provides reasons why they had the courage to undergo their sufferings. The most prominent motive in 2 Maccabees 7 is belief in the resurrection. The second son says that "the King of the universe will raise us up to an everlasting renewal of life, because we have died for his laws" (7:9). The third son offers his tongue and his hands since "I got these from Heaven, and because of his laws I disdain them, and from him I hope to get them back again" (7:11). The fourth son says: "One cannot but choose to die at the hands of men and to cherish the hope that God gives of being raised again by him. But for you there will be no resurrection to life" (7:14). The mother counsels the seventh son: "Accept death, so that in God's mercy I may get you back again with your brothers" (7:29).

We cannot be certain how widespread the idea of resurrection as the vindication of the just was in Palestinian Judaism during the crisis period. In Daniel 12:1-3 the coming of God's kingdom is to be accompanied by the resurrection of the dead, and so 2 Maccabees 7 may reflect a common approach. But 1 Maccabees makes no mention of such a belief. Moreover, the author of 2 Maccabees shows himself ready to discover belief in the resurrection where it may not have been (see 2 Macc 12:43-45). At any rate, the resurrection belief expressed in 2 Maccabees 7 has exercised an enormous influence on Jews and Christians throughout the centuries. In the midst of his catalogue of martyrdoms the author of 2 Maccabees gives his own interpretation in 6:12-16:

> [12]Now I urge those who read this book not to be depressed by such calamities, but to recognize that these punishments were designed not to destroy but to discipline our people. [13]In fact, not to let the impious alone for long, but to punish them immediately, is a sign of great kindness. [14]For in the case of the other nations the Lord waits patiently to punish them until they have reached the full measure of their sins; but he does not deal in this way with us, [15]in order that he may not take vengeance on us afterward when our sins have reached their height. [16]Therefore he never withdraws his mercy from us. Though he disciplines us with calamities, he does not forsake his own people.

His theology of these martyrdoms as divine discipline in the present allows him to preserve the identity of Israel as God's people while acknowledging the realities of suffering and death.

Before rejoining Judas Maccabeus in chapter 8 it may be useful to trace the course of events up to this point according to 2 Maccabees:

175: Jason outbids Onias III for the priesthood and imposes a program of forced Hellenization.

172: Menelaus outbids Jason for the priesthood and robs the temple vessels; Antiochus IV also robs the temple.

167: The temple cult is changed, and the persecutions and martyrdoms occur.

In this sorry state of affairs Judas Maccabeus arises as a champion for Israel. He and his companions first organize a force of about 6,000 men and undertake a series of guerrilla actions (8:5-7):

> [5]As soon as Maccabeus got his army organized, the Gentiles could not withstand him, for the wrath of the Lord

had turned to mercy. ⁶Coming without warning, he would set fire to towns and villages. He captured strategic positions and put to flight not a few of the enemy. ⁷He found the nights most advantageous for such attacks. And talk of his valor spread everywhere.

After Judas defeated Nicanor (8:8-29) as well as Timothy and Bacchides (8:30-33), even Nicanor acknowledges the threat to the Seleucids posed by Judas as God's instrument by proclaiming "that the Jews had a Defender (=God), and that therefore the Jews were invulnerable, because they followed the laws ordained by him" (8:36).

In 2 Maccabees (unlike 1 Maccabees) the death of Antiochus IV precedes the purification of the Jerusalem temple. The various stories about Antiochus's death are compared in chapter five. Here our interest is the outline of events according to 2 Maccabees 9. After being repulsed in Persia (9:1-4) and determined to attack Jerusalem, Antiochus is struck down by God with a foul disease (9:5-12). Recognizing this disease as "the scourge of God" (9:11), Antiochus vows to free the city of Jerusalem and even become a Jew (9:13-18). This is all very doubtful on the historical level; the one fact common to other sources is that Antiochus's death in Persia had some connection to his robbing a temple. Having appointed his son Antiochus V as his successor (9:19-27), Antiochus IV died (9:28-29).

The death of the persecutor sets the stage for the purification of the Jerusalem temple by Judas and his followers according to 10:1-8.

> ¹Now Maccabeus and his followers, the Lord leading them on, recovered the temple and the city; ²and they tore down the altars which had been built in the public square by the foreigners, and also destroyed the sacred precincts. ³They purified the sanctuary, and made another altar of sacrifice; then, striking fire out of flint, they offered sacrifices, after a lapse of two years, and they burned incense and lighted lamps and set out the bread of the Presence.
>
> ⁴And when they had done this, they fell prostrate and besought the Lord that they might never again fall into such misfortunes, but that, if they should ever sin, they might be

disciplined by him with forbearance and not be handed over to blasphemous and barbarous nations. [5]It happened that on the same day on which the sanctuary had been profaned by the foreigners, the purification of the sanctuary took place, that is, on the twenty-fifth day of the same month, which was Chislev. [6]And they celebrated it for eight days with rejoicing, in the manner of the feast of booths, remembering how not long before, during the feast of booths, they had been wandering in the mountains and caves like wild animals. [7]Therefore bearing ivy-wreathed wands and beautiful branches and also fronds of palm, they offered hymns of thanksgiving to him who had given success to the purifying of his own holy place.

[8]They decreed by public ordinance and vote that the whole nation of the Jews should observe these days every year.

The climax of the Antiochus IV episode is the purification of the temple and the establishment of Hanukkah as a festival. First the remnants of foreign worship are taken away, and the Jewish worship is restored to its proper forms (10:1-3). Then there is public prayer that this catastrophe never happen again (10:4). Next there is a description of Hanukkah (10:5-8): It begins on the same day as the desecration began, i.e., the twenty-fifth of Chislev (November-December); it is celebrated for eight days and is like the feast of booths; and the whole nation of Jews is to observe it every year.

There is a curious element to the Hanukkah account in 2 Maccabees. It concerns the reference to "ivy-wreathed wands" (10:7) carried in procession. That plus the reference to "wandering in the mountains and caves like wild animals" (10:6) leads the attentive reader to ask what precisely is going on here. These features were more appropriate to the cult of Dionysus than to an "orthodox" brand of Judaism (see 6:7). At any rate, the author of 2 Maccabees passes over these problems without comment, suggesting that at least for him these peculiar features could be interpreted in a way that was acceptable to traditional Jews.

Nicanor

The third major attack on the Jerusalem temple involves Judas Maccabeus and the Syrian general Nicanor. Before telling that incident the author of 2 Maccabees explains how Judas consolidated his power and defeated his enemies. Although the purification of the temple was surely an important symbolic event and marked an important stage in the Maccabean revolt, it was merely an initial step that needed to be filled out by other actions and victories.

After signalling the accession of Antiochus V Eupator (10:10-13), 2 Maccabees describes Judas's victories over the Idumeans (10:14-23), Timothy (10:24-38), and Lysias at Bethzur (11:1-15). There follow four pieces of correspondence: Lysias to the Jewish people (11:16-21), Antiochus to Lysias (11:22-26), Antiochus to the senate of the Jews and the Jewish people (11:27-33), and two Roman envoys to the Jewish people (11:34-38). The thrust of this correspondence is that the Jewish people be left in peace and be allowed to retain their ancestral customs.

With the advent of peace, the Jews went about their farming (12:1). But some Seleucid governors "would not let them live quietly and in peace" (12:2). Thus the shameful slaughter of 200 Jews at Joppa aroused Judas to take revenge (12:3-9) at Joppa and Jamnia. After defeating a force of Arabs (12:10-12), Judas attacked the fortified Gentile city of Caspin (12:13-16), captured Timothy and allowed his release (12:17-25), marched against Carnaim and the temple of Atargatis (12:29-31), and went up to Jerusalem for the feast of Pentecost (12:31). Then following Pentecost, he did battle against Gorgias (12:32-37). After assembling his army and celebrating the Sabbath (12:38), Judas went about burying his fallen comrades. In one of the most famous texts in 2 Maccabees (12:39-45), Judas discovers why these Jewish soldiers fell: The reason for their death was their wearing the sacred tokens of the idols of Jamnia under their tunics. The sin offering provided by Judas (12:43) was probably intended to avoid contaminating the living in Judas's army. But the author of 2 Maccabees takes it as proof of Judas's belief in the resurrection of the dead and the possibility of the living interceding on behalf of the dead:

[43]In doing this he acted very well and honorably, taking account of the resurrection. [44]For if he were not expecting that those who had fallen would rise again, it would have been superfluous and foolish to pray for the dead. [45]But if he was looking to the splendid reward that is laid up for those who fall asleep in godliness, it was a holy and pious thought. Therefore he made atonement for the dead, that they might be delivered from their sin.

The year 163 B.C. brings a new, all-out attack by Antiochus V and Lysias (13:1-2). At first the high priest Menelaus supported this attack. But when Antiochus V and Lysias realized that Menelaus was responsible for the situation, they had him executed. The author can hardly conceal his pleasure (13:3-8):

> [3]Menelaus also joined them and with utter hypocrisy urged Antiochus on, not for the sake of his country's welfare, but because he thought that he would be established in office. [4]But the King of kings aroused the anger of Antiochus against the scoundrel; and when Lysias informed him that this man was to blame for all the trouble, he ordered them to take him to Beroea and to put him to death by the method which is the custom in that place. [5]For there is a tower in that place, fifty cubits high, full of ashes, and it has a rim running around it which on all sides inclines precipitously into the ashes. [6]There they all push to destruction any man guilty of sacrilege or notorious for other crimes. [7]By such a fate it came about that Menelaus the lawbreaker died, without even burial in the earth. [8]And this was eminently just; because he had committed many sins against the altar whose fire and ashes were holy, he met his death in ashes.

The campaign of Antiochus V and Lysias was not successful. The king was attacked first by Judas near Modein (13:9-17) and defeated again by him near Beth-zur (13:18-22). The campaign was cut short by reports of revolt back in Antioch (13:23):

[23]Lysias got word that Philip, who had been left in charge of the government, had revolted in Antioch; he was dismayed, called in the Jews, yielded and swore to observe all their rights, settled with them and offered sacrifice, honored the sanctuary and showed generosity to the holy place.

Thus in 163 B.C. the Jews once more find themselves in a state of relative security.

Three years later (about 161 B.C.) things have changed: There is a new Seleucid king, Demetrius I (14:1-2); a new Jewish high priest, Alcimus; and a new threat to the Jerusalem temple in the person of Nicanor. Alcimus, "who had formerly been high priest but had willfully defiled himself in the times of separation" (14:3), tries to convince Demetrius I to take action against Judas Maccabeus on the grounds that "as long as Judas lives, it is impossible for the government to find peace" (14:10). In response the king appoints Nicanor governor of Judea and Alcimus the high priest (14:12-13).

When Nicanor arrives in Judea, he actually becomes a personal friend of Judas. The author suggests that there would have been peace in Judea if Alcimus had not reported to Demetrius I that Nicanor was plotting with Judas (14:26). Forced to do the king's bidding, Nicanor demands that Judas be handed over to him (14:33):

"If you do not hand Judas over to me as a prisoner, I will level this precinct of God to the ground and tear down the altar, and I will build here a splendid temple to Dionysus."

The threat against Judas also involves the threat against the temple.

The death of Razis (14:37-46), one of the elders of Jerusalem, is narrated as a kind of martyrdom (see 6:18-7:42). He is said to die "for Judaism" (14:38) and with hope in the resurrection of the dead (14:46.)

The battle with Nicanor is narrated in 2 Maccabees 15. Nicanor's plan to attack Judas and his men at Samaria on the Sabbath does not succeed (15:1-5). In exhorting his men before the final battle, Judas recounts a dream in 15:12-16.

12What he saw was this: Onias, who had been high priest, a noble and good man, of modest bearing and gentle manner, one who spoke fittingly and had been trained from childhood in all that belongs to excellence, was praying with outstretched hands for the whole body of the Jews. 13Then likewise a man appeared, distinguished by his gray hair and dignity, and of marvelous majesty and authority. 14And Onias spoke, saying, "This is a man who loves the brethren and prays much for the people and the holy city, Jeremiah, the prophet of God." 15Jeremiah stretched out his right hand and gave to Judas a golden sword, and as he gave it he addressed him thus: 16"Take this holy sword, a gift from God, with which you will strike down your adversaries."

He also makes a prayer in 15:22-24:

"O Lord, thou didst send thy angel in the time of Hezekiah king of Judea, and he slew fully a hundred and eighty-five thousand in the camp of Sennacherib. 23So now, O Sovereign of the heavens, send a good angel to carry terror and trembling before us. 24By the might of thy arm may these blasphemers who come against thy holy people be struck down."

When the battle is joined (15:25-27) the Jews succeed in "laying low no less than thirty-five thousand men" (15:27). Nicanor himself is slain. His corpse is recovered, and parts of it are exhibited as signs of his arrogance and God's power to protect the Jerusalem temple: "Blessed is he who has kept his own place undefiled" (15:34). There is a decree that Nicanor's Day—the thirteenth day of the twelfth month (Adar)—be observed (15:36).

The author of 2 Maccabees brings his story to an end in 161 B.C. with the defeat of Nicanor. He does so in the same engaging style as that of his prologue:

37This then is how matters turned out with Nicanor. And from that time the city has been in the possession of the Hebrews. So I too will here end my story. 38If it is well told and to the point, that is what I myself desired; if it is poorly done and mediocre, that was the best I could do. [39]For just as it is harmful to drink wine alone, or again, to drink water alone, while wine mixed with water is sweet and delicious and enhances one's enjoyment, so also the style of the story delights the ears of those who read the work. And here will be the end.

Conclusion

The second half of 2 Maccabees allows us to continue the outline of events in the Maccabean revolt:

164: The purification of the Jerusalem temple.
163: The campaign of Antiochus V and Lysias.
161: The defeat of Nicanor.

The value of 2 Maccabees as a historical source has already been discussed at the beginning of our analysis of the book. As we have seen, 2 Maccabees gives us many names and places in comparison with the book of Daniel. It differs from Daniel in highlighting tensions within the Jewish community at Jerusalem, especially with regard to the office of high priest. Whereas in Daniel the threat against the Jews comes mainly from outside, in 2 Maccabees the threat is the result of the combined efforts of Seleucids and Jews.

A final factor in assessing 2 Maccabees as a historical source concerns the distinction between the events (and Jason's presentation of them) and the author's interpretation of them. That tension came out in 2 Macc 12:39-45 where the author put forth Judas's provision for a sin offering as proof of his belief in the resurrection of the dead. A more serious tension involves the basic interpretation of the threat posed by Antiochus IV Epiphanes. The author of 2 Maccabees presents it as a systematic program of imposing the Greek way of life on Jews. Yet when he comes to describe what galvanized Jewish opposition to the program, he says that it was Menelaus's strategy of temple-robbing (see 4:32, 39). What then was the real nature of the threat: a religious-cultural program imposed by Antiochus IV, or the perfidious behavior of an illegitimate high priest? So in dealing with this source (and the other sources) we must be sensitive to the tensions between events and their interpretation, especially in writings from a culture in which events always received interpretations.

4

First Maccabees: God's Dynasty

1 Maccabees covers the events alluded to in Daniel and described in 2 Maccabees—and much more. Not only does it cover events up to 161 B.C., but it also continues the story down to the late second century B.C. The basic outline of the book reveals its purpose: After describing the crisis fomented by Antiochus IV Epiphanes (chap. 1) and the resistance sparked off by Mattathias (chap. 2), it recounts the exploits of Judas Maccabeus (3:1—9:22), his brothers Jonathan (9:23—12:53) and Simon (13:1—15:41), and Simon's son John Hyrcanus (chap. 16). The author wants to show how God used Judas and his brothers to remove the yoke of Seleucid oppression, and how the Jewish high priesthood came to reside in this family. Judas and his brethren represent God's dynasty. This purpose is vividly expressed in 1 Macc 5:61-62, when Joseph and Azariah try to gain military glory on their own and suffer defeat:

> 61Thus the people suffered a great rout because, thinking to do a brave deed, they did not listen to Judas and his brothers. 62But they did not belong to the family of those men through whom deliverance was given to Israel.

The subject matter of 1 Maccabees is the family raised up by God to deliver Israel. If 2 Maccabees can be called "temple propaganda," 1 Maccabees can be viewed as propaganda for the Hasmonean dynasty.

The text of 1 Maccabees is in Greek, part of the Septuagint.

Most scholars assume that 1 Maccabees was originally composed in Hebrew and then translated into Greek, though it is conceivable that it was composed in a Semitizing Greek. At any rate, the present text is written in "biblical Greek," much like the Greek versions of the early historical books of the Greek Bible 1 Maccabees ends with the exploits of John Hyrcanus, who was high priest from 134 to 104 B.C. The book may have been composed during the reign of John Hyrcanus or shortly thereafter (in the early first century B.C.). It incorporates some official documents (e.g., 8:23-32; 10:18-20; 10:25-45; 11:30-37; 11:57-59; 12:5-23; 13:36-40). The authenticity of these documents is disputed, though current scholarship tends to support them in the main. Of course, if 1 Maccabees was composed in Hebrew, then we are dealing with Greek documents translated into Hebrew and translated again back to Greek. Some scholars argue that 1 Maccabees and 2 Maccabees used a common source in their accounts of Judas Maccabeus (1 Maccabees 1-7; 2 Maccabees 3-15). That may be so. But it does not seem possible to recover this source, given the complicated transmissions of both books. The poems, speeches, and prayers are best seen as the free compositions of the author.

The focus of 1 Maccabees is God's dynasty—the priest Mattathias, his five sons (John, Simon, Judas, Eleazar, and Jonathan), and his grandson (John Hyrcanus). Whereas the book of Daniel looks for divine intervention soon to put Israel's enemies to flight and for the establishment of God's kingdom, 1 Maccabees presents the Maccabean dynasty as bringing about Israel's salvation. Whereas 2 Maccabees focuses on Judas in his role as savior of the Jerusalem temple, 1 Maccabees considers three generations of the Maccabean dynasty and attends to their military exploits as well as their ability to deal in the political arena. In its literary style the book seems anxious to link the Maccabean family with the great heroes of Israel's past. An important element in this program is the device of "biblical re-creations," that is, deliberate attempts at showing how the actions of the Maccabean dynasty stand in line with the words and deeds of the early heroes of the Hebrew Bible. The not-so-subtle message, of course, is that the

Maccabean dynasty carries on the heritage of Israel's past. The reading of 1 Maccabees presented here will give particular attention to the book's distinctive angle of viewing events in the second century B.C. Without making exhaustive comparisons with 2 Maccabees, it will note the differences between the two presentations of Judas Maccabeus. It will also show how events unfolded after 161 B.C., making clear that the Maccabean revolt did not end with the dedication of Jerusalem temple or the defeat of Nicanor.

Crisis

1 Maccabees begins by setting the scene for the emergence of Antiochus IV Epiphanes (1:1-10). It traces events back to Alexander the Great and his conquest of the Persian empire and gives a simplistic picture of the division of Alexander's kingdom. It accuses his successors of causing "many evils on the earth" (1:9). It finally brings Antiochus IV on stage in the 137th year of the kingdom of the Greeks (=175 B.C.)

Antiochus IV is the primary villain according to 1 Maccabees. Nevertheless there is a hint of Jewish cooperation in his program:

> [11]In those days lawless men came forth from Israel, and misled many, saying, "Let us go and make a covenant with the Gentiles round about us, for since we separated from them many evils have come upon us." [12]This proposal pleased them, [13]and some of the people eagerly went to the king. He authorized them to observe the ordinances of the Gentiles. [14]So they built a gymnasium in Jerusalem, according to Gentile custom, [15]and removed the marks of circumcision, and abandoned the holy covenant. They joined with the Gentiles and sold themselves to do evil.

The political intrigues spun by Simon, Jason, and Menelaus are summarized in two verses and a half (1:11-13a). No names or details are given. Some scholars argue that they have been omitted deliberately to avoid giving those "enemies within Israel" any prominence or notoriety. This device of *damnatio memoriae* was used in the Greco-Roman world and may be operative here. But the omission also reminds us that the author of 1 Maccabees was more interested in the exploits of his heroes than in explaining the threat facing Israel. The "program" of Antiochus and his Jewish conspirators is described in a succinct way (1:13b-15): observing a Gentile legal system (instead of the Torah!), building a gymnasium, removing the marks of circumcision, and abandoning the traditional Jewish religion ("the holy covenant"). Whether Jews actually underwent operations to cover up the marks of circumcision is questionable. The commentaries explain that such an operation was possible. But the reference in 1 Macc 1:15 may be rhetorical hyperbole, a kind of metaphor for abandoning the distinctive features of Judaism. Note that 1 Maccabees (unlike 2 Maccabees) does not describe this program as going over to the Greek way of life. Nor does it give much motivation beyond the idea that, when Jews abandon their separation, things will go better for them (1:11).

At this point Antiochus IV becomes the chief enemy of Israel. After his successful invasion of Egypt in 169 B.C. and defeat of Ptolemy VI Philometor, Antiochus returns by way of Jerusalem and robs sacred vessels from the temple (1:21-24):

> [21]He arrogantly entered the sanctuary and took the golden altar, the lampstand for the light, and all its utensils. [22]He took also the table for the bread of the Presence, the cups for drink offerings, the bowls, the golden censers, the curtain, the crowns, and the gold decoration on the front of the temple; he stripped it all off. [23]He took the silver and the gold, and the costly vessels; he took also the hidden treasures which he found. [24]Taking them all, he departed to his own land.

Note that there is no mention of the insurrection begun by Jason or the high priest Menelaus serving as Antiochus IV's guide.

In 167 B.C. Antiochus sends a "chief collector of tribute" (perhaps the leader of Mysian troops) against Jerusalem (1:29-40), and he establishes within Jerusalem a citadel (1:33-35):

³³Then they fortified the city of David with a great strong wall and strong towers, and it became their citadel. ³⁴And they stationed there a sinful people, lawless men. These strengthened their position; ³⁵they stored up arms and food, and collecting the spoils of Jerusalem they stored them there, and became a great snare.

This citadel will enjoy a remarkably long existence. It ceased to exist in 141 B.C., under Simon (see 1 Macc 13:49-50). The identity of the "sinful people, lawless men" (1:34) is disputed: Were they Gentiles, heterodox Jews, supporters of Menelaus, or a mixture of such groups? At any rate, for over twenty-five years the citadel remained in non-Maccabean hands and served as the center for opposition to the Maccabean revolt. In my opinion the best way of marking the success of the Maccabean revolt and determining its end is the removal of the enemy troops from the citadel in Jerusalem.

The precise location of the citadel in Jerusalem is disputed. But the lament attached to the description of the citadel's founding (1:36-40) suggests that it was near the Jerusalem temple: "It became an ambush against the sanctuary..." (1:36).

Having robbed the temple vessels and established a citadel near the temple, Antiochus issues a decree that threatens to erase the distinctive features of Judaism and bring Jews into the "mainstream" of his empire (1:41-50):

> ⁴¹Then the king wrote to his whole kingdom that all should be one people, ⁴²and that each should give up his customs. ⁴³All the Gentiles accepted the command of the king. Many even from Israel gladly adopted his religion; they sacrificed to idols and profaned the sabbath. ⁴⁴And the king sent letters by messengers to Jerusalem and the cities of Judah; he directed them to follow customs strange to the land, ⁴⁵to forbid burnt offerings and sacrifices and drink offerings in the sanctuary, to profane sabbaths and feasts, ⁴⁶to defile the sanctuary and the priests. ⁴⁷to build altars and sacred precincts and shrines for idols, to sacrifice swine and unclean animals, ⁴⁸and to leave their sons uncircumcised. They were to make themselves abominable by everything

unclean and profane, [49]so that they should forget the law and change all the ordinances. [50]And whoever does not obey the command of the king shall die.

The description first portrays Antiochus's program as a kind of religious-cultural ecumenism (1:41-42): "that all should be one people." The problem with this description is that such a program of religious-cultural ecumenism does not fit in the ancient world in general or with the behavior of Antiochus IV in particular. Note again that there is no mention of going over to "the Greek way of life" as in 2 Maccabees. There is talk about going over to the king's religion (1:43), suggesting that the cult to be promoted instead of Yahweh worship will be oriental in character.

The directives aimed at the Jews (1:44-49) concern the abolition of many of the distinctive features of Judaism in the Second Temple period: the temple service and its system of sacrifices, observance of the Sabbath and Jewish holy days, circumcision of male children, and the laws of ritual purity. Moreover, the animals to be sacrificed in the temple are pigs and other ritually unacceptable animals. The effect of these prohibitions and directives would destroy the distinctive features of Second Temple Judaism and thus efface Jewish identity as a distinct people.

The decree was implemented in 167 B.C. not only in Jerusalem but also in the countryside (1:51-53). The most dramatic step was taken at the Jerusalem temple where "they erected a desolating sacrilege upon the altar of burnt offering" (1:54). Elsewhere in Judah altars were built and incense burned (1:54-55). Another dramatic step was the destruction of the books of the Jewish Law and the condemnation of anyone who possessed them or adhered to them. Still another measure was taken against women who had their sons circumcised; the infants were hung from their mother's necks, and both mother and son destroyed. These steps regarding temple worship, the Law, and circumcision are presented as part of a deliberate effort by Antiochus IV Epiphanes to change the Jews by destroying Judaism.

The Jewish response to the program is mixed. On the one hand, "many of the people, every one who forsook the law, joined them, and they did evil in the land" (1:52). On the other hand, there emerges the beginning of a Jewish resistance movement: "they drove Israel into hiding in every place of refuge they had" (1:53). Note that the opponents of Antiochus's program are identified as Israel, with the implication that its Jewish supporters no longer belong to Israel. The martyrs are acknowledged but passed over quickly in 1:62-64:

> [62]But many in Israel stood firm and were resolved in their hearts not to eat unclean food. [63]They chose to die rather than to be defiled by food or to profane the holy covenant; and they did die. [64]And very great wrath came upon Israel.

Some scholars argue that the author of 1 Maccabees did not think highly of martyrs and even considered them to be fools. While such an interpretation goes beyond the evidence, it does bring out the fact that the author was more concerned with the leadership that the pious in Israel would get from the Maccabees than with the heroic sufferings of the Jewish martyrs. At this point in the narrative they are only the seed of resistance by the pious opposition. For that opposition to flower it must receive solid and bold leadership. It will get such leadership from the family of Mattathias, the son of John, the son of Simeon (2:1).

Resistance

Having described the crisis facing Jews under Antiochus IV, the author of 1 Maccabees recounts the beginning of organized resistance in 166 B.C. under the leadership of Mattathias, from the priestly family of the sons of Joarib. The resistance took shape at Modein, a town about seventeen miles north-west of Jerusalem. Mattathias is said to have moved there from Jerusalem. Whether he had moved there in response to the crisis or some years before is impossible to decide from the text (2:1). The five sons of Mattathias, who constitute the focus of attention throughout 1 Maccabees, are listed in 2:2-5: John (see 9:35-42), Simon (see 13-15), Judas (see 3:1-9:22), Eleazar (see 6:40-47), and Jonathan (see 9:23-12:53). Mattathias and his descendants are sometimes called the "Maccabees" after the nickname given to Judas (probably meaning "the hammer"). They are also sometimes known as the "Hasmoneans," perhaps in connection with Simeon the grandfather of Mattathias.

The cause for the resistance was the blasphemy committed against the temple and holy city of Jerusalem. Mattathias expresses his sorrow and anger in a lament (2:7-13), and then he and his sons go into mourning. The lament runs as follows:

> "Alas! Why was I born to see
> this,
> the ruin of my people, the ruin
> of the holy city,
> and to dwell there when it was
> given over to the enemy,
> the sanctuary given over to aliens?
> [8] Her temple has become like a man
> without honor,
> [9] her glorious vessels have been
> carried into captivity.
> Her babes have been killed in her
> streets,
> her youths by the sword of the
> foe.
> [10] What nation has not inherited her
> palaces
> and has not seized her spoils?
> [11] All her adornment has been taken
> away;
> no longer free, she has become
> a slave.
> [12] And behold, our holy place, our
> beauty,
> and our glory have been laid
> waste;
> the Gentiles have profaned it.
> [13] Why should we live any longer?"

The occasion for the resistance was the arrival at Modein of officers from the king who had orders to make the people there offer sacrifice according to the "new order." The officers address Mattathias in public and promise him and his sons generous rewards to be the first in the town to do "as all the Gentiles and the men of Judah and those that are left in Jerusalem have done" (2:18). These arguments fail to convince Mattathias, who answers according to 2:19-22:

> [19]But Mattathias answered and said in a loud voice: "Even if all the nations that live under the rule of the king obey him, and have chosen to do his commandments, departing each one from the religion of his fathers, [20]yet I and my sons and my brothers will live by the covenant of our fathers.[21]Far be it from us to desert the law and the ordinances. [22]We will not obey the king's words by turning aside from our religion to the right hand or to the left."

Mattathias follows words of resistance with an act of resistance (2:23-26). When a Jew comes forward to sacrifice, Mattathias killed not only the Jew but also the king's officer and tore down the altar. In line with the theme of biblical "re-creation" his display of zeal for the law is compared with that of Phinehas against Zimri (see Num 25:6-15). Then he invites everyone who "is zealous for the law and supports the covenant" to flee with him and his sons to the hills.

This incident involving Mattathias and his sons is not even mentioned in 2 Maccabees (see 5:27). There is no certain explanation. The incident may have been unknown or seemed unimportant to the author of 2 Maccabees. Or it may have been used as Hasmonean propaganda and even blown out of its historical proportion by the author of 1 Maccabees. The effect in 1 Maccabees is that the beginning of the revolt is pinpointed to an action undertaken by Mattathias and to a tiny movement whose nucleus was constituted by his five sons. The aim of 1 Maccabees is to trace how that small movement quickly became "Israel" and supplied its champions.

First a momentous decision about attitude and strategy must be taken (2:29-41). That decision will distance the Maccabees from the scrupulously pious who insist on Sabbath-observance over self-defense. These pious persons had gone off to the wilderness to avoid the evils that had befallen Jerusalem. When their pursuers caught up with them and attacked them on the Sabbath, they refused to resist. They said: "Let us all die in our innocence; heaven and earth testify for us that you are killing us unjustly" (2:37). The result was the death of a thousand persons (2:38).

The same incident was narrated briefly in 2 Macc 6:11: "Others who had assembled in the caves nearby, to observe the seventh day secretly, were betrayed to Philip and were all burned together, because their piety kept them from defending themselves, in view of their regard for that most holy day." The incident may also be echoed in the story of Taxo and his seven sons in *Testament of Moses.* The way in which the group is described suggests some relation to the community that gave us eventually the Dead Sea scrolls: "any who were seeking righteousness and justice went down there to the wilderness to dwell there" (2:29).

Whatever the precise identity of this pious group may be, their fate leads Mattathias and his friends to determine not to follow their example. If they were to do so, Israel's enemies would soon annihilate them. Therefore they decide to defend themselves when attacked on the Sabbath day: "Let us fight against every man who comes to attack us on the Sabbath day; let us not all die as our brethren died in their hiding places" (2:41).

This decision having been taken, the Maccabees are joined by a company of Hasideans ("pious ones"). The fact that they are described as "mighty warriors of Israel" (2:42) would seem to distinguish them from those who were killed because they refused to fight on the Sabbath. At this point the resistance gains further definition: The organized army strikes down sinners and lawless men, tears down pagan altars, circumcises uncircumcised boys, and hunts down arrogant men (2:44-47). Their success is summarized as follows: "They rescued the law out of the hands of the Gentiles and kings, and they never let the sinner gain the upper hand" (2:48).

The first stage of the Maccabean revolt reaches its climax with the death of Mattathias and the text of his testament. After urging his sons to show zeal for the law and give their lives for the covenant, he invokes a series of biblical models, thus contributing to the device of biblical "re-creation" (2:51-60):

> [51]"Remember the deeds of the fathers, which they did in their generations; and receive great honor and an everlasting name. [52]Was not Abraham found faithful when tested, and it was reckoned to him as righteousness? [53]Joseph in the time of his distress kept the commandment, and became lord of Egypt. [54]Phinehas our father, because he was deeply zealous, received the covenant of everlasting priesthood. [55]Joshua, because he fulfilled the command, became a judge in Israel. [56]Caleb, because he testified in the assembly, received an inheritance in the land. [57]David, because he was merciful, inherited the throne of the kingdom for ever. [58]Elijah because of great zeal for the law was taken up into heaven. [59]Hananiah, Azariah, and Mishael believed and were saved from the flame. [60]Daniel because of his innocence was delivered from the mouth of the lions.

That the author knew the book of Daniel (or at least the stories contained in chaps 3 and 6) is indicated by the references to Hananiah, Azariah, and Mishael (2:59) and to Daniel (2:60). Mattathias foretells Antiochus IV's fall ("his splendor will turn into dung and worms," 2:62), appoints Simon counsellor but Judas commander of the army (2:65-66), and urges his sons to "pay back the Gentiles in full and heed what the law commands" (2:68). His death take place in 166 B.C., and he is buried at Modein.

Judas

The leadership exercised by Judas Maccabeus is described in 1 Maccabees 3:1—9:22. His career is covered not only down to 161 B.C. (as in 2 Maccabees) but even to his death in 160 B.C. He is primarily a daring military leader.

After introducing Judas (3:1-2) and quoting a poem celebrating his exploits (3:3-9), 1 Maccabees explains how Judas defeated Apollonius (governor of Samaria) and took his sword (3:10-12). Judas's first major victory takes place at Beth-horon (twelve miles northwest of Jerusalem) over Seron, the commander of the Syrian army (3:13-26). In view of his small army Judas could hardly have been expected to win over Seron. In true biblical fashion, Judas explains: "It is not on the size of the army that victory in battle depends, but strength comes from heaven" (3:19).

Though Antiochus IV wished to pursue the campaign against Judea, he found himself in need of money and went off to Persia to raise funds (3:27-31). He left Lysias in charge of his affairs and gave him orders to destroy Jerusalem (3:32-37). He departed from Antioch in 165 B.C. But Antiochus's plans for destroying Judea are thwarted by Judas and his army. Judas defeats Lysias's generals Gorgias and Nicanor at Emmaus (3:38—4:25) and then Lysias himself at Beth-zur (4:26-35). Recall that according to 2 Macc 8:8-36 Judas's initial victories were over Nicanor, Timothy, and Bacchides. How these two accounts can be harmonized is hard to know.

The cause for which Judas and his army fight in these initial successes is "our people and the sanctuary" (3:43). Two poems portray the present evil state of the temple as symbolic of the evil state of the people. The first (3:45) is the lament of the congregation:

> 45Jerusalem was uninhabited like a
>   wilderness;
>   not one of her children went in
>   or out.
> The sanctuary was trampled down,
>   and the sons of aliens held the
>   citadel;
>   it was a lodging place for the
>   Gentiles.
> Joy was taken from Jacob;
>   the flute and the harp ceased to
>   play.

The second (3:51-53) sums up a day of fasting and mourning at Mizpah, opposite Jerusalem:

⁵¹Thy sanctuary is trampled down
  and profaned,
  and thy priests mourn in
  humiliation.
⁵²And behold, the Gentiles are
  assembled against us to
  destroy us; thou knowest
  what they plot against us.
⁵³How will we be able to withstand
  them,
  if thou dost not help us?

The device of biblical "re-creation" is also present in these accounts. Judas scrupulously observes the regulations laid down in Deuteronomy 20:5-8 and dismisses those who were building houses or were betrothed or were planting vineyards or were faint-hearted (3:56). In addressing his troops before battle Judas compares them to the exodus generation: "Remember how our fathers were saved at the Red Sea, when Pharaoh with his forces pursued them" (4:9). On their return from victorious battle the soldiers sing hymns and praises to "Heaven" (=God; 1 Maccabees prefers this substitute for the divine name, as Matthew did also)—"for he is good, for his mercy endures forever" (4:24). The next year (164 B.C.) when Lysias himself mounted a campaign against Judas and his army, the two forces met at Beth-zur (4:26-35). In his prayer before battle Judas invokes another biblical precedent: "Blessed art thou, O Savior of Israel, who didst crush the attack of the mighty warrior (=Goliath) by the hand of thy servant David and didst give the camp of the Philistines into the hands of Jonathan, the son of Saul, and of the man who carried his armor" (4:30). Judas gains another victory, and Lysias retreats with the vow to invade Judea with an even larger army.

The first phase of Judas's leadership reaches its climax with the re-dedication of the Jerusalem temple (4:36-61). On going up to Mount Zion, Judas and his men find the temple in shambles (4:38). (Why it should be in disrepair if it were being used for pagan rites is not explained.) The citadel is still in enemy hands (4:41). And so Judas sends a detail to fight off the troops there until he had cleansed the sanctuary. The story of the cleansing of the temple is told in 1 Macc 4:42-51:

> [42]He chose blameless priests devoted to the law, [43]and they cleansed the sanctuary and removed the defiled stones to an unclean place. [44]They deliberated what to do about the altar of burnt offering, which had been profaned. [45]And they thought it best to tear it down, lest it bring reproach upon them, for the Gentiles had defiled it. So they tore down the altar, [46]and stored the stones in a convenient place on the temple hill until there should come a prophet to tell what to do with them. [47]Then they took unhewn stones, as the law directs, and built a new altar like the former one. [48]They also rebuilt the sanctuary and the interior of the temple, and consecrated the courts.
> [49]They made new holy vessels, and brought the lampstand, the altar of incense, and the table into the temple. [50]Then they burned incense on the altar and lighted the lamps on the lampstand, and these gave light in the temple. [51]They placed the bread on the table and hung up the curtains. Thus they finished all the work they had undertaken.

Then on the twenty-fifth of Chislev in 164 B.C., on the anniversary of the temple's profanation the people began the eight-day celebration of Hanukkah. Judas, his brothers, and the assembly determine that the feast of the Dedication should be celebrated every year for eight days, beginning on the twenty-fifth day of the ninth month (4:59). Instituting a feast in commemoration of an event of very recent experience was a Hellenistic custom. It is ironic that the group portrayed in the major Jewish sources as the champions of traditional Judaism against the inroads of Hellenism should be responsible for instituting a feast that had no biblical warrant and that this feast should be celebrated to the present day.

The end of the first phase of Judas's leadership found him in control of the Jerusalem temple and environs and the fortress of Beth-zur (about twenty miles south of Jerusalem). In the second phase Judas and his companions attack in all directions: Idumea to the south (5:3-5, 65), Ammon and Gilead east of the Jordan (5:6-13, 24-51), Galilee to the north (5:21-23), and the coastal plain. Their attacks are presented as in revenge for past harm visited on Jews in these territories or to ward off the threat of destruction there. Those who act outside of the leadership of the Maccabees (5:55-62, 67) suffer defeat, whereas Judas and his brothers are greatly honored in all Israel and among the Gentiles (5:63).

The death of Antiochus according to 1 Macc 6:1-17 will be discussed with its parallel accounts on pp. 97-103. Here it is enough to note that his death is presented *after* the dedication of the temple, not *before* it as in 2 Macc 9:1-29. The occasion for his death is his frustration at not succeeding in robbing a temple in Persia (6:1-4).

What disturbs him even more is the news about the Jewish victories over his troops (6:5-7). He traces the defeats to the evils that he did in the Jerusalem temple (6:12-13):

> 12But now I remember the evils I did in Jerusalem. I seized all her vessels of silver and gold; and I sent to destroy the inhabitants of Judah without good reason. 13I know that it is because of this that these evils have come upon me; and behold, I am perishing of deep grief in a strange land.

After appointing his "friend" (a technical term for the inner circle of advisers to the king) Philip to serve as regent until his son Antiochus V Eupator might reach maturity, Antiochus IV Epiphanes dies in the Seleucid year 149 (=163 B.C.). Thus a power struggle has been set up between two contenders for the regency: Lysias (see 3:32) and Philip (6:14-15).

The death of Antiochus IV Epiphanes did not bring peace and security for Judea, not as long as the citadel of enemy troops remained in Jerusalem: "Now the men in the citadel kept hemming Israel in around the sanctuary. They were trying in every way to harm them and strengthen the Gentiles" (6:18). Judas's siege of the citadel in 162 B.C. was successful (see 6:60-63). Some escapees from the citadel challenged the new king to do something about Judas and his movement. The way they speak suggests that those who manned the citadel were Jews (6:22-27):

> 22They went to the king and said, "How long will you fail to do justice and to avenge our brethren? 23We were happy

to serve your father, to live by what he said and to follow his commands. ²⁴For this reason the sons of our people besieged the citadel and became hostile to us; moreover, they have put to death as many of us as they have caught, and they have seized our inheritances. ²⁵And not against us alone have they stretched out their hands, but also against all the lands on their borders. ²⁶And behold, today they have encamped against the citadel in Jerusalem to take it; they have fortified both the sanctuary and Beth-zur; ²⁷and unless you quickly prevent them, they will do still greater things, and you will not be able to stop them."

But as we will see in 6:60-63, the citadel will soon revert to the Seleucids and cause further problems for the Jews. The Maccabean movement will not have really succeeded until this citadel is defeated. And that will occur only in 141 B.C. (see 13:51).

The complaints of the escapees lead to a new campaign against Judas. At Beth-zur the Jews repell an enemy attack (6:31), only to lose the place later on because they lacked supplies (6:48-54). Meanwhile at Beth-zechariah (6:32-47) in a battle featuring the use of elephants the first of the five brothers dies. Eleazar saw that one elephant was equipped with royal armor and assumed that it bore the king (6:43). As he stabbed the elephant from beneath, he was crushed by it and killed (6:46). Just as the Jewish cause seemed in danger the rivalry between the regents Lysias and Philip flared. When Lysias heard that Philip had come to Antioch and threatened to seize control of the government (6:56), he quickly came to peace terms with the Jews, agreeing "to let them live by their laws as they did before" (6:59). Part of the agreement is that the Jews will evacuate the citadel (6:61). But Lysias and Antiochus V break their oath, destroy the Jewish defenses at the temple, and presumably garrison more troops in the citadel (6:62). Then they return to Antioch and win back control of it from Philip. So the year 162 B.C. ends with the Maccabean movement in trouble. One brother is dead. There have been military defeats. The present peace is an uneasy one. The Seleucid king and his regent have weakened the Jewish defenses.

In the next year (161 B.C.) there is a new Seleucid king and a new Jewish high priest. Antiochus V Eupator and Lysias were slain at the command of Demetrius I Soter (162-150 B.C.), the son of Seleucus IV. Demetrius had replaced his uncle Antiochus IV as a hostage at Rome. In 161 he managed to escape by sea and return to Antioch. He seized the royal palace and had his army kill Antiochus V and Lysias (7:1-4). Alcimus, a claimant to the Jewish high priesthood, brought accusations against Judas and his brothers (7:5-7). The new king sent Alcimus and Bacchides to take vengeance on Israel. He also appointed Alcimus as the high priest (7:9). Their peaceful words did not fool Judas and his brothers (7:10). Thus far the story in 1 Maccabees 7 parallels that in 2 Maccabees 14.

There seems to have been a desire on the part of some in Israel to come to terms with Alcimus (and through him with Bacchides and Demetrius I). That desire was soon blunted by the unfortunate fate of some trusting Jews (7:12-18):

> 12Then a group of scribes appeared in a body before Alcimus and Bacchides to ask for just terms. 13The Hasideans were the first among the sons of Israel to seek peace from them, 14for they said, "A priest of the line of Aaron has come with the army, and he will not harm us." 15And he spoke peaceable words to them and swore this oath to them, "We will not seek to injure you or your friends." 16So they trusted him; but he seized sixty of them and killed them in one day, in accordance with the word which was written,
> 17"The flesh of thy saints and their
>   blood
> they poured out round about
>   Jerusalem,
> and there was none to bury them."
> 18Then the fear and dread of them fell upon all the people, for they said, "There is no truth or justice in them, for they have violated the agreement and the oath which they swore."

After a while Bacchides left Alcimus in charge of Judea and returned to Antioch (7:20). As Alcimus strengthened his position and gained further support, he recognized that Judas remained his major obstacle. His accusations against Judas led Demetrius to send Nicanor (7:26). Whereas in 2 Maccabees Nicanor goes through a period of friendly relations with Judas, in 1 Maccabees he seems to have been treacherous from the start (7:27-30). His threat to burn up the temple unless Judas is handed over (7:35) leads to battle against Judas, with Nicanor the first to fall (7:43). Judas's prayer before battle (7:41-42) carries on the motif of biblical re-creation (see 2 Kings 19:35):

> [41]"When the messengers from the king spoke blasphemy, thy angel went forth and struck down one hundred and eighty-five thousand of the Assyrians. [42]So also crush this army before us today; let the rest learn that Nicanor has spoken wickedly against thy sanctuary, and judge him according to this wickedness."

His prayer is answered, and the thirteenth of Adar becomes another day to be celebrated every year. Thus ends the parallelism between 1 Maccabees and 2 Maccabees.

1 Maccabees 8 is devoted to relations between Judas and the Romans (who had taken increasing interest in Seleucid and Ptolemaic areas of dominance). By entering into an alliance with Rome, the Maccabees gained a powerful protector against their more immediate enemies. They also took the first step toward dependence on a foreign power, a dependence that would become stronger and stronger through the first century B.C. and the first century A.D.

After a survey of Roman military achievements in the early second century B.C. and some inaccurate remarks on Roman institutions (8:1-16), 1 Maccabees recounts how emissaries were sent by Judas to Rome to make a treaty (8:17-22). Their proposal was accepted, and the text appears in 1 Macc 8:23-32. There has been a longstanding debate about the authenticity of the treaty. But most scholars today take it seriously as representing the basic agreement made between Judas's emissaries and the Romans:

> [23]"May all go well with the Romans and with the nation of the Jews at sea and on land for ever, and may sword and

enemy be far from them. [24]If war comes first to Rome or to any of their allies in all their dominion, [25]the nation of the Jews shall act as their allies wholeheartedly, as the occasion may indicate to them. [26]And to the enemy who makes war they shall not give or supply grain, arms, money, or ships, as Rome has decided; and they shall keep their obligations without receiving any return. [27]In the same way, if war comes first to the nation of the Jews, the Romans shall willingly act as their allies, as the occasion may indicate to them. [28]And to the enemy allies shall be given no grain, arms, money, or ships, as Rome has decided; and they shall keep these obligations and do so without deceit. [29]Thus on these terms the Romans make a treaty with the Jewish people. [30]If after these terms are in effect both parties shall determine to add or delete anything, they shall do so at their discretion, and any addition or deletion that they may make shall be valid. [31]And concerning the wrongs which King Demetrius is doing to them we have written to him as follows, 'Why have you made your yoke heavy upon our friends and allies the Jews? [32]If now they appeal again for help against you, we will defend their rights and fight you on sea and on land.'"

Both sides agree to be an ally to the other in war and not to supply the other's enemy. Whether the warning in 8:31-32 was part of the treaty is debated. Josephus omits it. And in fact the Romans did not do anything to help the Jews against Demetrius I. Yet there is evidence that the Romans were never really very scrupulous about fulfilling their obligations in this kind of treaty. They acted usually when it best suited their own interests. On the other hand, a small constituency like the Maccabees had little to lose from such a treaty. Its existence might scare off the Seleucids, who would not know whether this might be one of those cases that might bring about Roman intervention. It also gave the Maccabees and their supporters the status of speaking on behalf of Israel and so constituting the government.

In 160 B.C. Demetrius sent Bacchides and Alcimus to make still another attack against Jerusalem. This time their forces outnumber Judas's army: 20,000 foot soldiers and 2,000 cavalry against 3,000. The odds are so bad that many in Judas's army desert, with the result that only 800 are left to fight (9:6). After a courageous effort, Judas fell in battle (9:18). His burial is narrated in the style of the biblical books of Kings, and the lament over him is a quotation from 2 Sam 1:19:

> [19]Then Jonathan and Simon took Judas their brother and buried him in the tomb of their fathers at Modein, [20]and wept for him. And all Israel made great lamentation for him; they mourned many days and said,
> [21]"How is the mighty fallen,
>   the savior of Israel!"
> [22]Now the rest of the acts of Judas, and his wars and the brave deeds that he did, and his greatness, have not been recorded, for they were very many.

Thus the theme of biblical "re-creation" that has carried through the career of Judas draws that career to a close. Once more the Maccabean movement finds itself in serious trouble. It desperately needs a new leader and a new way of dealing with its enemies. It will find both in the person of Jonathan, the brother of Judas.

Jonathan

Whereas Judas Maccabeus was a brilliant and daring military leader, his brother Jonathan was a skillful politician. At first he was a military leader only and then on from time to time. But his greatest success came from playing off one claimant to the Seleucid throne against another, and thus gaining territory and security for his people. From one perspective the Maccabean revolt was over with Judas's death. What gave it new life was Jonathan's political skill.

The state of affairs after Judas's death was grim: A great famine occurred, many went over to the enemy, Bacchides put the "ungodly" in charge of the country, and he persecuted the "friends" of Judas (9:23-26). Against the background of this "great distress in Israel" (9:27) the "friends" of Judas chose Jonathan as their ruler and leader (9:28-31). While fleeing from pursuit by Bacchides (9:32-34), Jonathan is betrayed by the Nabatean sons of Jambri from Medeba who seize his brother John and put him to death (9:36, 38). Now three brothers have died. Jonathan and Simon get revenge by ambushing a wedding party and return to the marshes of the Jordan (9:37-42). Although Jonathan managed to elude his trap at the Jordan River (9:43-49), Bacchides seems to have under control most of Judea and has taken hostage the sons of the leading men at the citadel (9:50-53).

In 159 B.C. Alcimus began to tear down the inner wall of the sanctuary, thus giving access to pagans to areas intended for Jews (9:54). But Alcimus suffered a stroke and died in great agony (9:55-56). Thereafter Bacchides returned to Antioch and left Judea at rest for two years (9:57). Two years later (157 B.C.) certain "lawless men" convinced Bacchides to try to destroy Jonathan and Simon. When he failed to do so, he came to terms with the surviving Maccabees. Jonathan takes on the role of the ancient judges (9:73):

> 73Thus the sword ceased from Israel. And Jonathan dwelt in Michmash. And Jonathan began to judge the people, and he destroyed the ungodly out of Israel.

The "Maccabean revolt" seems to have reached a standstill between 157 B.C. and 152 B.C. What revived the movement was the arrival of Alexander Balas (or Alexander Epiphanes), who presented himself as the son of Antiochus IV Epiphanes (10:1). His appearance constituted a real threat to Demetrius I, who now needed as many allies as he could muster. Thus Jonathan found himself in the enviable position of being courted by both Demetrius I and Alexander Balas. As a skillful politician Jonathan played one's promises off against the other's and had the ability to discern whose word might be trusted. Moreover, Jonathan seems to have been the only Jewish leader available with whom Demetrius and Alexander could deal. After the death of Alcimus in 159 B.C. there is no mention of a high priest. Perhaps the Seleucids decided after all their troubles with Jason, Menelaus, and Alcimus that the office of high priest should remain vacant. The period between 159 and 152 B.C. when there was no high priest in Jerusalem is sometimes called the *intersacerdotium* ("between priesthood[s]").

The first offer to Jonathan comes from Demetrius, who allows Jonathan to raise an army and commands that the hostages in the citadel be released (10:6). This move allowed Jonathan to move back to Jerusalem and take control of it and the places previously held by Bacchides (10:10-14).

The next offer came from Alexander Balas, who offers to appoint Jonathan the Jewish high priest and to be the king's "friend" (i.e., one of his special counsellors) (10:18-20):

> [18]"King Alexander to his brother Jonathan, greeting. [19]We have heard about you, that you are a mighty warrior and worthy to be our friend. [20]And so we have appointed you today to be the high priest of your nation; you are to be called the king's friend" (and he sent him a purple robe and a golden crown) "and you are to take our side and keep friendship with us."

So at the feast of Tabernacles in 152 B.C. Jonathan "put on the holy garments" (10:21) as high priest and recruited an even larger army.

The third offer comes from Demetrius (10:25-45). It is a kind of "wish list" for a small people like the Jews: exemption from taxes, handing over the citadel, release of Jewish captives, permission to celebrate holidays, the right to be part of the king's army, annexation of more territory, support for services at the temple, permission for asylum at the temple, and funds for rebuilding the temple and the city ways. But Jonathan and the people found Demetrius's promises too good to be true, and so they sided with Alexander (10:47). They were wise to do, since shortly thereafter Demetrius was killed in battle (10:50). When Alexander arranges a marriage alliance with the Ptolemies, Jonathan is later summoned to meet with the two kings and emerges wearing purple and bearing the titles of general and governor of the province (10:65).

In 147 B.C. Demetrius II, the son of Demetrius I, challenged Alexander and began a new round of political involvement with respect to Jonathan. When challenged to battle by Apollonius, Jonathan and Simon gain possession of Joppa

(10:74-76), burn Azotus (10:77-85), and gain booty from Askalon (10:86-87). The result is even more honor from Alexander Balas (10:88-89). But Alexander was undone by his own father-in-law, Ptolemy VI. Just as Alexander had been slain (11:17), three days later Ptolemy VI died. So Demetrius II became king in 145 B.C. by default.

While political affairs were confused, Jonathan assembled an army to attack the citadel still another time (11:20). Summoned to a conference at Ptolemais, Jonathan won Demetrius II over, had himself confirmed as high priest and friend of the king (11:27), and even came away with some of the items on the "wish list" from Demetrius I (11:30-37).

Just as Demetrius II seemed to have matters under control, he sparked off a rebellion by dismissing native soldiers in favor of his own foreign troops (11:38-40). At this moment Jonathan made a formal request that Seleucid troops be withdrawn from various strongholds and especially from the citadel in Jerusalem (11:41). In return Jonathan was asked to supply 3,000 troops of his own to help put down the rebellion (11:42-44). The Jewish troops performed magnificently (11:45-51), but Demetrius II failed to keep his part of the bargain (11:52-53).

In 145 B.C. Antiochus IV Epiphanes, the son of Alexander Balas, through the agency of Trypho, ousted Demetrius II and gained control of Antioch. He immediately confirmed Jonathan's privileges (11:57) and made Simon the governor of the coastal territory from the Ladder of Tyre to the borders of Egypt (11:59). These privileges gave the brothers scope for more military activity at Gaza, Kadesh in Galilee, and Hazor.

Willing to accept privileges from the Seleucid rulers but not content to be totally dependent on them, Jonathan sent a delegation to Rome to renew the treaty made under Judas (see 1 Maccabees 8). He also began communication with the Spartans on the basis of an earlier communication between the Jewish high priest Onias I (320-290 B.C.) and the Spartan king Arius (308-265 B.C.), and an alleged relationship between the two peoples (12:5-23).

The struggle for the Seleucid throne was not over, and Jonathan and Simon found themselves drawn into it (12:24-34). In a series of measures aimed at strengthening their own

positions they try to isolate the citadel from the rest of
Jerusalem so that its garrison could neither buy nor sell
(12:36). When Trypho sought to push aside Antiochus VI and
become king himself (12:39), he tried to eliminate Jonathan.
At Beth-shan (12:40-45) Trypho backed away from battle with
Jonathan but at Ptolemais (12:46-48) trapped Jonathan and
took him captive (12:50). Thus ended the public career of
Jonathan, a brilliant politician and strategist. His skillful
dealings rescued the "Maccabean revolt" from defeat and did
much to make the people of Israel an independent nation
again.

Simon

From its very beginning (166 B.C.) Simon had been part of
the Maccabean movement. Now in 142 B.C. he was the only
one of the five brothers capable of leading Israel. Eleazar,
Judas, and John had been killed. Jonathan had been captured.
According to 1 Macc 13:1-11 Simon volunteered to lead the
people of Israel. Their response was to acclaim Simon their
leader: "You are our leader in place of Judas and Jonathan
your brother. Fight our battles, and all that you say to us we
will do" (13:8-9).

Trypho moved to invade Judea and decided to use Jonathan
as a hostage. He claimed to be holding Jonathan for payment
of taxes (13:15) and demanded a hundred talents of silver and
two of his sons in exchange for Jonathan (13:16). If Simon
refused to act on this matter, it might appear that he was only
interested in seizing power for himself. But he knew that
Trypho would not keep his part of the bargain. And he did not.
Frustrated by a heavy snowstorm from linking up with the
men in the citadel (13:21), Trypho went off to Gilead and killed
Jonathan (13:23) on his way back to Antioch. When Simon
recovered the body of Jonathan, he buried him at Modein and
erected a monument to the Maccabean family (13:27-30):

> [27]And Simon built a monument over the tomb of his
> father and his brothers; he made it high that it might be seen,
> with polished stone at the front and back. [28]He also erected

seven pyramids, opposite one another, for his father and mother and four brothers. [29]And for the pyramids he devised an elaborate setting, erecting about them great columns, and upon the columns he put suits of armor for a permanent memorial, and beside the suits of armor carved ships, so that they could be seen by all who sail the sea. [30]This is the tomb which he built in Modein; it remains to this day.

When Trypho killed Antiochus VI and became king in his place, Simon renewed contact with Demetrius II and gained a favorable reply (13:36-40) in which all privileges were renewed and all offenses were pardoned. Since Demetrius really did not have power, the favorable reply was not very significant. But the author of 1 Maccabees made 142 B.C. into the beginning of an era in 13:41:

> [41]In the one hundred and seventieth year the yoke of the Gentiles was removed from Israel, [42]and the people began to write in their documents and contracts, "In the first year of Simon the great high priest and commander and leader of the Jews."

Simon combined in his person the religious leadership ("the great high priest"), military leadership ("commander"), and political leadership ("leader of the Jews)".

After taking control of Gazara (literally Gaza, but most likely Gezer), Simon finally was able to gain domination over the citadel at Jerusalem (13:49-52). So in 141 B.C. the great symbol of the incompleted character of the Maccabean revolt passed into Simon's control:

> [49]The men in the citadel at Jerusalem were prevented from going out to the country and back to buy and sell. So they were very hungry, and many of them perished from famine. [50]Then they cried to Simon to make peace with them, and he did so. But he expelled them from there and cleansed the citadel from its pollutions. [51]On the twenty-third day of the second month, in the one hundred and seventy-first year, the Jews entered it with praise and palm

branches, and with harps and cymbals and stringed
instruments, and with hymns and songs, because a great
enemy had been crushed and removed from Israel. [52]And
Simon decreed that every year they should celebrate this
day with rejoicing. He strengthened the fortifications of the
temple hill alongside the citadel, and he and his men dwelt
there.

Chapter 13 ends with a note introducing John Hyrcanus, the
son of Simon, who is being groomed to succeed his father
(13:53).

The movement led by Demetrius II came to a halt in 140
B.C. when he was captured by Arsaces, the king of Persia and
Media (14:1-3). Nevertheless the reign of Simon is peaceful
enough. Indeed the poem presented in 1 Macc 14:4-15 portrays
it as an idyllic period and uses traditional images from the
Hebrew Bible, thus picking up the device of biblical
"re-creation":

[4]The land had rest all the days of
　　Simon.
　He sought the good of his
　　nation;
　his rule was pleasing to them,
　　as was the honor shown him, all
　　his days.
[5]To crown all his honors he took
　　Joppa for a harbor,
　and opened a way to the isles of
　　the sea.
[6]He extended the borders of his
　　nation,
　and gained full control of the
　　country.
[7]He gathered a host of captives;
　he ruled over Gazara and
　　Beth-zur and the citadel,
　and he removed its uncleanness
　　from it;
　and there was none to oppose

him.
8They tilled their land in peace;
  the ground gave its increase,
  and the trees of the plains their
    fruit.
9Old men sat in the streets;
  they all talked together of good
    things;
  and the youths donned the
    glories and garments of war.
10He supplied the cities with food,
  and furnished them with the
    means of defense,
  till his renown spread to the ends
    of the earth.
11He established peace in the land,
  and Israel rejoiced with great joy.
12Each man sat under his vine and
    his fig tree,
  and there was none to make
    them afraid.
13No one was left in the land to fight
    them,
  and the kings were crushed in
    those days.
14He strengthened all the humble of
    his people;
  he sought out the law,
  and did away with every lawless
    and wicked man.
15He made the sanctuary glorious.
  and added to the vessels of the
    sanctuary.

After this poem, 1 Maccabees 14 presents information about
how both the Romans and the Spartans confirmed their
alliances with Simon (14:16-24). It also presents a decree of
appreciation for Simon's benefactions to the people of Israel
(14:27-45) in which Simon is officially proclaimed as leader,
high priest, and governor (14:41-42). The official character of

this decree is indicated by its inscription on bronze tablets, its posting in the sanctuary, and the deposit of copies in the treasury. With the end of the citadel in Jerusalem and the official recognition of Simon's claim to the high priesthood, military leadership, and political power, the Maccabean revolt had gone far beyond what anyone in Israel could have imagined in 165 B.C.

Although Simon had achieved stability in Judea, the Seleucid dynasty had none. In 138 B.C. Simon received a letter from Antiochus VII Sidetes, the son of Demetrius I and younger brother of Demetrius II. In that letter (15:2-9) Antiochus VII proposed to seize the Seleucid throne from Trypho, reconfirmed Simon's privileges, and promised him and his people great honors when the successful outcome of the coup was reached. But as the military action against Trypho proceeded, Antiochus VII rejected Simon's help and demanded that Simon return the conquered cities and lands of Judea to him as the Seleucid ruler (15:28-31). Simon's reply comes in 1 Macc 15:33-35:

> "We have neither taken foreign land nor seized foreign property, but only the inheritance of our fathers, which at one time had been unjustly taken by our enemies. [34]Now that we have the opportunity, we are firmly holding the inheritance of our fathers. [35]As for Joppa and Gazara, which you demand, they were causing great damage among the people and to our land; for them we will give a hundred talents."

After Trypho's departure (15:37), the Seleucid general Cendebeus attempted to provoke and attack the Jews but was thwarted by John Hyrcanus (15:38—16:10). The dynastic history comes to a close in 16:11-22 with the story of Simon's death and the accession of John Hyrcanus. Simon was killed in 134 B.C. while drunk at a banquet at the stronghold of Dok near Jericho. His son-in-law, Ptolemy the son of Abubus, sought to seize Simon's domain by doing away with Simon and his sons (16:13). He did manage to kill Simon and two of his sons (16:16) but failed to kill John Hyrcanus (16:19), who survived the attack against him.

1 Maccabees breaks off very early in the reign of John Hyrcanus (134-104 B.C.). It ends (16:23-24) as the reports about the kings of ancient Israel and Judah do in the canonical books of Kings:

> 23The rest of the acts of John and his wars and the brave deeds which he did, and the building of the walls which he built, and his achievements, 24behold, they are written in the chronicles of his high priesthood, from the time that he became high priest after his father.

The "chronicles of his high priesthood" have been lost.

Historical Value

1 Maccabees is clearly the most important historical resource for studying the Maccabean revolt. It allows us to fill out the chronological table begun with the help of Daniel and 2 Maccabees:

160: Judas killed in battle; Jonathan acclaimed as his successor.

159: The high priest Alcimus dies; the priesthood remains open until 152.

152: Alexander Balas replaces Demetrius I and appoints Jonathan high priest.

142: Jonathan dies; Simon replaces him.

134: Simon is killed; his son John Hyrcanus succeeds him.

The style of 1 Maccabees is generally straightforward and factual in comparison with the allusive book of Daniel and the dramatic 2 Maccabees. Where parallel passages exist between 1 Maccabees and 2 Maccabees, there are some puzzling discrepancies. And it is hard to judge which source is the more reliable on the whole. But 1 Maccabees at least gives the appearance of reliability.

The appearance of historical reliability should not distract from the rather narrow perspective of 1 Maccabees, which views all events in relation to Mattathias and his five sons. It attributes to them the beginning of resistance to Antiochus IV. It follows their military and political activities. It rejects the idea that others in Israel could succeed apart from them (see 5:61-62). It comes close to equating them with the "true Israel" and rejects their opponents as "lawless men."

First Maccabees is aptly called "dynastic history." It provides the history of a dynasty through three generations—from Mattathias to John Hyrcanus. Its narrow focus on one family would allow the descendants of that family to ground their own claims to religious, military, and political power in Israel. If 2 Maccabees deserves the title "temple propaganda," 1 Maccabees deserves the title "dynastic propaganda."

5

Anatomy of
the Maccabean Revolution

The preceding chapters have traced the course of the Maccabean revolution with the help of the three principal literary sources for it. Reading these sources in the order Daniel—2 Maccabees—1 Maccabees has enabled us to develop a narrative of events spread over more than forty years. But in these presentations we have seen also that each source views the events from a peculiar angle. According ot the book of Daniel, the arrogance of the Seleucid king Antiochus IV would be broken by the coming of God's kingdom. 2 Maccabees stresses God's care for the Jerusalem temple and his use of Judas Maccabeus as a divine instrument. 1 Maccabees views the entire historical period as dominated by the Maccabean dynasty.

What really happened? That is the question to be answered by historians. It is seldom an easy question to answer. Even with regard to modern events for which there is abundant written material and eyewitness testimony it is often hard to determine with certainty what really happened. By whom and why was John F. Kennedy assassinated? What was behind the "Watergate" and "Irangate" affairs? If the question is hard to answer with respect to contemporary events, it is clearly much harder to be sure about events of over two-thousand years ago for which we possess only a few, rather tendentious literary sources, written in an age in which "objective" reporting was not a major value. Nevertheless, the sources at our disposal do at least allow us to develop an outline of major events and to follow the course of the Maccabean revolt. With that outline secure, we can return to some of the problems that the sources present to the historian.

Outline of Events

The events described in Daniel, 2 Maccabees, and 1 Maccabees took place against the background of Seleucid history in general and the Seleucid kingship in particular. Many of the decisive events occurred around the shift of emperors. The sequence of Seleucid rulers runs as follows:

223-187:	Antiochus III
187-175:	Seleucus IV Philopator
175-164:	Antiochus IV Epiphanes
163-162:	Antiochus V Eupator
162-150:	Demetrius I Soter
150-145:	Alexander I Balas
145-139:	Demetrius II Nicator
145-142:	Antiochus VI (and Trypho)
138-129:	Antiochus VII Sidetes

A chart can help illustrate their family relationships:

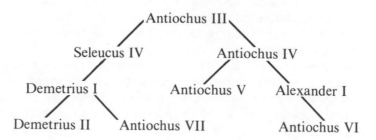

The Seleucid kingship bounced back and forth among the descendants of Antiochus III. That dynastic struggle formed the backdrop for the Maccabean revolution.

In *The Anatomy of Revolution* (revised and expanded version; New York: Vintage, 1965), Crane Brinton supplied the following definition of revolution: "the drastic, sudden substitution of one group in charge of the running of a territorial political entity by another group hitherto not running that government " (p. 4).

From one perspective the Maccabean revolt was not very remarkable. At the beginning the province of Judea was administered by the high priest Onias III under the oversight of a Seleucid governor (see 2 Macc 3:1-3, 5). At the end Judea was ruled by the Maccabean high priest John Hyrcanus. The chief difference was the increase in Jewish political independence from the Seleucids that the Maccabees gained. But from another perspective that increase in political independence was enormously significant. The Jews of Palestine had gone from being a small client people first in the Ptolemaic and then in the Seleucid empires to being an independent political entity tied by treaties to the Romans and the Spartans. They gained control over large areas of the land of Israel and rekindled their sense of national identity dormant since the exile of 587 B.C.

From the sources analyzed in the preceding chapters it is possible to distill an outline of the principal events in the Maccabean revolution. The sources, of course, focus on this or that event in the list. But the following occurrences seem pivotal for grasping the course of events:

175: Antiochus IV Epiphanes as Seleucid king.
175-172: Jason as Jewish high priest.
172-163: Menelaus as high priest.
169: Antiochus IV's first Egyptian campaign, followed by plunder of Jerusalem temple.
168: Antiochus IV's second Egyptian campaign, founding of the citadel in Jerusalem.
167: Desecration of Jerusalem temple and persecution of Jews.
165: Judas leads the revolt.
164: End of persecution, dedication of temple.
162: Alcimus as Jewish high priest.
161: Judas's victory over Nicanor and alliance with the Romans.
160: Death of Judas, accession of Jonathan.
159: Death of Alcimus.
152: Jonathan as Jewish high priest.
142: Death of Jonathan, accession of Simon.
141: Conquest of the Jerusalem citadel.
134: Death of Simon, accession of John Hyrcanus.

In the analysis of revolutions it is a truism that the first stages of a revolution are not always clear to the revolutionaries. From the perspective of hindsight and as part of his dynastic history the author of 1 Maccabees placed the beginning of the revolt in 166/5 at Modein with the bold action of Mattathias and his five sons (see 1 Maccabees 2). The author of 2 Maccabees attributes leadership to Judas (see 2 Macc 5:27; 8:1-7) but says little about his brothers and nothing about the incident at Modein. Daniel may dismiss the Maccabean movement as "a little help" (Dan 11:34).

From another perspective one could trace the beginnings of the Maccabean revolt back to the high priesthoods of Jason and Menelaus. Their buying the high priesthood introduced a note of instability into Palestinian Jewish life and tied the temple service into the political power struggle. In 2 Maccabees Jason is portrayed as a "Hellenizer" and Menelaus as an unscrupulous temple robber turned traitor. The "revolution" could conceivably have stopped during the high priesthood of either Jason (175-172 B.C.) or Menelaus (172-163 B.C.). That it did not was surely due to the leadership of Judas and the instincts of his Jewish supporters.

Not all Israel supported the Maccabean revolt. Even though 1 Maccabees tends to equate the Maccabean movement with Israel and to dismiss other Jews as "lawless men," it is clear that there were several parties besides the Maccabees. Both Jason and Menelaus had Jewish supporters. The pious observers of the Sabbath and the Hasideans were two more groups outside the Maccabean circle. At least some of the troops garrisoned in the citadel seem to have been Jews.

The course of the Maccabean revolt was neither smooth nor quick. Judas and his band had dramatic military successes at the start, probably due to their familiarity with the land and its people. The capture of the Jerusalem temple and the restoration of the temple service there (the first Hanukkah) solidified the movement and gave it credibility. The symbolic significance of Maccabean control of the temple must have been very powerful. It is still powerful—so much so that many modern readers assume that the revolt had reached its successful conclusion with the dedication of the temple.

The ancient sources tell a different story, one of further

attacks against Judas and Jerusalem, of defeats in battle, and of deaths. With the death of Judas in 160 B.C. and the arrival of Alcimus as the Jewish high priest it looked as if the "Maccabean" revolt was finished. And finished it was until 152 B.C. when Jonathan got into a bidding war among the claimants to the Seleucid throne. Skillfully playing one against the other and joining political shrewdness with military daring, Jonathan and Simon managed to gain control of the religious, military, and political affairs of their people.

The seven-year vacancy of the high priesthood (*intersacerdotium*) from 159 B.C. (the death of Alcimus) to 152 B.C. (Jonathan's appointment) was the occasion for the revival of the Maccabean movement. Since the rival claimants to the Seleucid throne needed allies and since Jonathan seems to have been the closest thing around to an official spokesman for Israel, Jonathan and Simon were able to resurrect a movement that appeared spent. The *intersacerdotium* probably created the climate in which Jonathan's accession to the high priesthood was generally acceptable. The Maccabees were from a priestly family ("the sons of Joarib," see 1 Macc 2:1; 1 Chr 24:7; Neh 11:10). But the priesthood should have remained among the family of Onias III (see 2 Maccabees 3-4). Much about what went on during the period from 159 to 152 B.C. is unclear. At the end, however, the author of 1 Maccabees could describe Jonathan's accession to the Jewish high priesthood without explanation or apology.

Just as it is difficult to pinpoint the beginning of a revolution, it is also hard to know when one is over. A successful revolution results in a stable government and a restoration of civil life. The transition from revolution to the new order is vague, precisely because one phase blends into the other. One clear marker for the beginning and the end of the Maccabean revolt is the fate of the citadel in Jerusalem. From its founding in 168 B.C. to its dissolution in 141 B.C. it was a remarkably hardy and persistent institution. The citadel was a fortress in Jerusalem. It must have been close to the temple area. It was manned by troops loyal to the Seleucid rulers and governors. Some of the troops may have been Jewish, some may have been Syrians or Gentile inhabitants of the land of Israel. The citadel survived an amazingly long time (twenty-seven years) and caused the Maccabees a good deal of trouble. Only when the citadel was dissolved (see 1 Macc 13:50), could the revolution undertaken by the Maccabees be called a real success.

Revolutions often sow the seeds of their own destruction. One such seed was the reliance on Rome as a protector. Though the Romans were eager to make treaties but slow to follow through on them unless it suited their own interests, the treaties between the Romans and Jews did exist because Judas, Jonathan, and Simon entered into relationship with the Romans. There was now an official link between the two peoples. The official link suited both parties in the short run. The Jews had a powerful protector against the Seleucids and Ptolemies. The Romans had in their client state of Judea a foothold in the Middle East.

Another seed of destruction was the concentration of power in the Maccabean dynasty. Though such concentration was probably necessary if the revolution was to succeed, the result was that one family had all the religious, political, and military power. And that family soon fell victim to the dynastic struggles that plagued the Seleucids and Ptolemies. The two seeds of destruction came together in 63 B.C. when the Roman general Pompey settled a Hasmonean family dispute about who was to be the successor of Salome Alexandra.

Careful analysis of Daniel, 2 Maccabees, and 1 Maccabees allows the historian to sketch the general outline of the Maccabean revolt and to speak about its character, beginning and end, and other matters. But these sources refuse to answer some important questions: Why did Antiochus IV Epiphanes persecute the Jews? Why did Antiochus IV die? Did the authors of 2 Maccabees and 1 Maccabees use a common source in describing Judas's defeat of Nicanor? Attention to these questions will illustrate some problems in studying the Maccabean revolution.

The Persecution

One obvious problem in dealing with the literary sources for the Maccabean revolt is that they do not always tell us all that we want to know. These books were written more than two-thousand years ago. They do not share our modern idea of history as trying to determine what really happened. They seldom focus on the causes of movements or events; when they do supply causes, modern readers are likely to be disappointed at the explanations.

A case in point is the "persecution" of the Jews under Antiochus IV Epiphanes. The sources are surprisingly weak in supplying information about the details and the causes of this persecution. It is explained as just punishment for the people's sins in Daniel 9, or as divine discipline for their sins in 2 Macc 6:12-16, or as the result of Antiochus IV's arrogance in 1 Maccabees 1. Modern readers may agree that there could be some truth in these moralistic explanations. But most of us find them too familiar, too vague, and too "religious."

What happened to the Jews of Palestine is sometimes described as the first religious persecution, that is, the first attempt by a ruler to destroy a religion by destroying its faithful adherents. This is an attractive idea, one that puts these events in the realm of modern experience with respect to the Nazi Holocaust or other horrors. But there are problems with such a description. First, the ancients did not think of "religion" as an independent segment of life, separable from cultural, economic, political, and social realities. Furthermore, the idea of a "religious" persecution was foreign to the people of antiquity, who generally allowed native cultures to continue while performing a kind of translation and integration of them into the more dominant religion. Finally, nothing known from other sources about Antiochus IV Epiphanes indicates that he would have been responsible for such a "religious" persecution. Though often erratic in his personal behavior, Antiochus IV was a student of Epicurean philosophy and a patron of various religious shrines.

The "moralistic" explanations for the persecution are unsatisfying. The "first religious persecution" idea carries with it some serious problems. This is the point at which the modern historian enters. The modern historian must deal with documentary evidence, but also must sift through that evidence in order to find out more than may be on the surface of the sources. The classic modern historical study of the persecution under Antiochus IV Epiphanes is Elias Bickerman's *The God of the Maccabees: Studies on the Meaning and Origin of the Maccabean Revolt.*

Bickerman described his task as "a purely historical one . . . to determine the sequence of events we usually call the persecution of Antiochus, and to make this series of events comprehensible." His conclusion (and the basic thesis of his entire study) was that the Maccabean movement was primarily part of a civil war, a religious struggle between reformers and orthodox, which posterity has remembered as a war against the Seleucids. According to Bickerman, the "persecution" had its roots in a Jewish quarrel about religion.

Whatever merits Bickerman's basic thesis may have, it has been very influential and is often brilliant in its details. Bickerman gave serious attention to texts that hint at inner-Jewish conflicts. For example, Dan 11:32 speaks of those who "violate the covenant" being seduced by Antiochus. And 1 Macc 1:11 describes certain "lawless men" who misled many by saying: "Let us go and make a covenant with the Gentiles round about us, for since we separated from them many evils have come upon us." Even more fertile for grasping the inner-Jewish conflict are those texts in 2 Maccabees that describe the machinations of Jason and Menelaus. In Bickerman's perspective, Jason and Menelaus were religious reformers who wished to "reform" Judaism, to make it less foreign and less particularistic. He compares them to the pioneers of the Jewish reform movement in the 1840s who proposed the abolition of the dietary laws and declared circumcision not to be binding.

There were two phases in the "religious reform." The milder phase, which took place under Jason (175-172), involved replacing the Torah as the law of the Jewish people (2 Macc 4:10-11) and the introduction of the gymnasium (2 Macc 4:12-15). The more severe phase came under Menelaus and his followers (172-163), who instigated the religious repression that was intended to abolish Jewish particularism.

Under Menelaus the Jerusalem temple became the temple of Olympian Zeus (2 Macc 6:2). It would be a grave error to assume that classical Greek religion was practiced in the Jerusalem temple, despite the mention of Olympian Zeus. The epithet is probably the "Greek interpretation" of the traditional

description of Israel's God as the "God of the heaven." The
Semitic term for "God of the heaven" was Baal Shamin. With
that expression in mind we can clear up the meaning of the
expression "abomination of desolation" (see Dan 11:31; 12:11;
also 9:27). The Hebrew for "abomination of desolation" (or
more literally "detested thing causing horror") is *šîqqûs
(mě)šômêm*. The phrase is a pun or word play in which *šîqqûs*
("detested thing") substitutes for "Baal" and *(mě)šômêm*
substitutes for "Shamin" ("heavens"). What is described by the
term was not a statue or image but rather some kind of sacred
stone erected on the altar of burnt offering (see 1 Macc 1:54).
Moreover, the reference to cultic prostitution (see 2 Mac 6:4)
confirms that the Jerusalem temple was not used for Greek
religion.

The God worshipped at the Jerusalem temple remained the
same—the God of the heavens, the God of Israel, whose Greek
equivalent was Olympian Zeus. What changed was the nature
of the worship, which became more assimilated to that of the
surrounding Semitic peoples. Bickerman summarized his
argument with the claim that three points had been established:
(1) The new order of worship was entirely un-Greek; (2) it
retained the veneration of the God of the Jews, (3) who,
however, in the form of his revelation and in the form of his
worship, was now equated with the divinities of the neighboring
peoples, the Syrians and the Arabs.

The thesis about the Semitic (rather than Greek) character
of the new order of worship is generally accepted by scholars.
But not all agree with Bickerman's explanation of the
persecution in terms of a "religious reform" instigated by Jason
and Menelaus and supported by Antiochus IV Epiphanes.
Others prefer to view the conflict in terms of social classes
(Tcherikover) or politics and economics (Bringmann).

According to Viktor Tcherikover, Hellenism in Jerusalem
was bound up with the wealthy families of the Jerusalem
aristocracy. Jason had received permission from Antiochus IV
to convert Jerusalem into a Greek city (*polis*) to be called
Antioch (see 2 Macc 4:9). This radical scheme led to a revolt by
the common people under the Hasideans against the Jewish
aristocracy. Antiochus's persecution was a response to the
revolt of the common people. The citadel was set up for the

Seleucid (Syrian) soldiers, and the new order of worship in the Jerusalem temple was simply the native cult of those soldiers. The Maccabees got into the struggle late and introduced the innovation of waging war on the Sabbath.

Klaus Bringmann takes a political-economic approach, i.e., the "persecution" was really about political power and money. Antiochus IV was primarily interested in consolidating his own power and assuring a secure source of income in the land of Israel. He needed these as part of his overall plan to turn his kingdom into a "second Rome."

Jason's bid for the high priesthood (see 2 Macc 4:7-8) appealed to Antiochus IV mainly because he promised more money. Jason's program of Hellenization (gymnasium, honorary Antiochian citizenship, etc.) would have posed no real offense to Judaism (despite what the author of 2 Maccabees says). Menelaus outbid Jason and gained the high priesthood on the promise of even more taxes (see 2 Macc 4:23-24). He raised the tax money by plundering the Jerusalem temple (see 2 Mac 4:32). In the face of the "religious" opposition aroused by Menelaus's plundering the temple (see 2 Macc 4:39-42), Menelaus convinced Antiochus IV to turn the Jerusalem temple into a Syrian-Canaanite shrine of Baal-Shamin (the god of the non-Jewish soldiers in the citadel) and to issue his "religious edict" (see 1 Macc 1:41-50) proscribing traditional Judaism. The goal was to put down the religious opposition and so to secure Antiochus's power and source of money. This disastrous miscalculation on the part of Menelaus and Antiochus IV had the effect of galvanizing Jewish opposition. The decree was later interpreted as an attempt to impose a Greek way of life on the Jews.

These exercises in historical detective work by Bickerman, Tcherikover, and Bringmann stress different aspects or causes of the persecution: religious, social, and political-economic. But they agree in tracing the persecution to tensions within the Jewish community, limiting the "persecution" to Jews in Jerusalem and Judea, identifying the Semitic character of the new order of worship, and affirming that the new order was both supported and opposed by Jews. These "historical detectives" have helped us to read the texts more carefully, since their chief findings are most certainly present in the texts.

Whereas these three interpreters trace the persecution to tensions within the Jewish community, Jonathan Goldstein focuses on Antiochus IV Epiphanes. Antiochus had been a hostage at Rome from 189/88 to 176/75 (see 1 Macc 1:10). According to Goldstein, the program of Antiochus should be understood as an attempt to imitate Roman civic and religious programs. Therefore Antiochus granted to some Jews honorary Antiochian citizenship (analogous to honorary Roman citizenship) and allowed Jason to draw up the list of those people of Jerusalem who were to be enrolled as Antiochians (see 2 Macc 4:9). He also wished to repress "traditional" Jewish religion and to substitute what he perceived as a restored, incorrupt cult of the God of the Jews. The "abomination of desolation" featured meteor stones (i.e., stones from heaven). The new cult would make the Jews like the Syrians and Phoenicians. Thus Goldstein attributes the persecution to the grandiose scheme of Antiochus to make his Seleucid empire into a second Rome.

The Death of Antiochus

Another set of problems facing the historian of the Maccabean revolt concerns the abundance of contradictory sources. An extreme example is provided by the four different biblical accounts of the death of Antiochus IV. Two of these appear in the same book, 2 Maccabees. Is it possible to sift through these accounts and arrive at what really happened?

Rather than beginning with the biblical narratives, we may find some extrabiblical reports about the death of Antiochus IV a better starting point. The Greek historian Polybius, whose work is an important resource for studying the rise of Roman power in the third and second centuries B.C., describes the death of Antiochus IV in the following way (31:9):

> In Syria King Antiochus, wishing to provide himself with money, decided to make an expedition against the sanctuary of Artemis in Elymais. On reaching the spot he was foiled in his hopes, as the barbarian tribes who dwelt in the neighborhood would not permit the outrage, and on his

retreat he died at Tabae in Persia, smitten with madness, as some people say, owing to certain manifestations of divine displeasure when he was attempting this outrage on the above sanctuary.

Polybius's account contains some elements that will run through most of the other sources: The occasion for Antiochus IV's death was his attempt at robbing a temple in Persia. Even though Polybius claims that Antiochus was "smitten with madness" and died in retreat at Tabae, he traces Antiochus's death to the "divine displeasure" at his efforts to rob the sanctuary of Artemis.

The death of Antiochus IV is also described by Appian (11:66): "[Antiochus] robbed the temple of Venus of Elymais; he then died of a wasting disease, leaving a son nine years of age..." Although Appian reports that Antiochus was robbing a temple, he disagrees with Polybius in two points: Antiochus IV died of a "wasting disease" rather than madness, and no clear causal connection is drawn between the temple-robbing and the death.

The second prefixed letter in 2 Maccabees contains an account of Antiochus's death something like those in the classical sources. According to 2 Macc 1:13-17, Antiochus IV was killed *while* robbing a temple of Nanea in Persia:

> [13]For when the leader reached Persia with a force that seemed irresistible, they were cut to pieces in the temple of Nanea by a deception employed by the priests of Nanea. [14]For under pretext of intending to marry her, Antiochus came to the place together with his friends, to secure most of its treasures as a dowry. [15]When the priests of the temple of Nanea had set out the treasures and Antiochus had come with a few men inside the wall of the sacred precinct, they closed the temple as soon as he entered it. [16]Opening the secret door in the ceiling, they threw stones and struck down the leader and his men, and dismembered them and cut off their heads and threw them to the people outside. [17]Blessed in every way be our God, who has brought judgment upon those who have behaved impiously.

The name of the goddess changes from Venus to Artemis to Nanea. But this change presents no real problem, since the names are really synonyms. The place—Persia—remains the same; Elymais was part of the Persian empire. The chief difference here is the immediate relation between Antiochus IV's temple robbing and his death. He died in the act of temple robbing, not sometime later as Polybius (with causal connection) and Appian (without causal connection) have it.

The main text of 2 Maccabees reports the death of Antiochus IV in quite a different way. According to 2 Maccabees 9, Antiochus had been unsuccessful in his attempt at robbing temples in the Persian city of Persepolis and was forced to retreat (9:1-2). While in Ecbatana he received word that Nicanor and Timothy had been defeated by the Jews (9:3). Angered by the news and frustrated by his defeat, Antiochus determined to make Jerusalem a "cemetery of Jews" (9:4). Before he could carry out this plan (9:5-7):

> [5]But the all-seeing Lord, the God of Israel, struck him an incurable and unseen blow. As soon as he ceased speaking he was seized with a pain in his bowels for which there was no relief and with sharp internal tortures—[6]and that very justly, for he had tortured the bowels of others with many and strange inflictions. [7]Yet he did not in any way stop his insolence, but was even more filled with arrogance, breathing fire in his rage against the Jews, and giving orders to hasten the journey. And so it came about that he fell out of his chariot as it was rushing along and the fall was so hard as to torture every limb of his body.

Thus Antiochus IV suffers from a wasting disease and the effects of a severe fall. But his illness brings him to his senses, according to 9:9-12:

> [9]And so the ungodly man's body swarmed with worms, and while he was still living in anguish and pain, his flesh rotted away, and because of his stench the whole army felt revulsion at his decay. [10]Because of his intolerable stench no one was able to carry the man who a little while before had thought that he could touch the stars of heaven. [11]Then it

> was that, broken in spirit, he began to lose much of his
> arrogance and to come to his senses under the scourge of
> God, for he was tortured with pain every moment. [12]And
> when he could not endure his own stench, he uttered these
> words: "It is right to be subject to God, and no mortal
> should think that he is equal to God."

This recognition leads to a series of promises by Antiochus IV
(9:14-17): Jerusalem will be a free city, Jews are to be equal to
citizens of Athens, the temple will be restored at the king's
expense, and he will become a Jew. There is no indication that
Antiochus IV did any of these things or even thought seriously
of them. His coming to recognition sounds much like the
recognition motif in the book of Daniel where the pagan king
acknowledges the power of the God of Israel.

Antiochus IV's sufferings do not abate (9:18), and so he
makes provision for his son Antiochus V to succeed him. The
text of the letter from Antiochus IV (9:19-27) sounds authentic;
it fits so poorly in 2 Maccabees 9 that it leaves the impression of
having been dropped into the chapter without too much
thought or editing. The cool and self-possessed mood of the
letter yields to the narrator's fury in 9:28: "So the murderer and
blasphemer, having endured the most intense suffering, such
as he had inflicted on others, came to the end of his life by a
most pitiable fate, among the mountains in a strange land."

So according to 2 Maccabees 9, Antiochus's temple-robbing
expedition in Persia was merely the occasion for his illness and
death. The cause of his death was his arrogance toward the
Jerusalem temple and the Jewish people. He recognized the
power of Israel's God and his own errors—but too late. He
died *before* the dedication of the Jerusalem temple, which
appears in 2 Macc 10:1-8 as a fitting sequel to the death of
Antiochus.

According to 1 Maccabees, Antiochus IV died (6:1-16) *after*
the dedication of the Jerusalem temple (4:36-61). As in 2
Maccabees 9, the occasion is temple robbing in Persia (6:1-4).
Frustrated by his unsuccessful efforts at robbing the temple in
Elymais, Antiochus fled back to Babylon. There he received
the news from Judea (6:5-7):

⁵Then some one came to him in Persia and reported that the armies which had gone into the land of Judah had been routed; ⁶that Lysias had gone first with a strong force, but had turned and fled before the Jews; that the Jews had grown strong from the arms, supplies, and abundant spoils which they had taken from the armies they had cut down; ⁷that they had torn down the abomination which he had erected upon the altar in Jerusalem; and that they had surrounded the sanctuary with high walls as before, and also Beth-zur, his city.

It was the bad news from Judea that made Antiochus IV sick according to 1 Macc 6:10-13:

> ¹⁰So he called all his friends and said to them, "Sleep departs from my eyes and I am down hearted with worry. ¹¹I said to myself, 'To what distress I have come! And into what a great flood I now am plunged! For I was kind and beloved in my power.' ¹²But now I remember the evils I did in Jerusalem. I seized all her vessels of silver and gold; and I sent to destroy the inhabitants of Judah without good reason. ¹³I know that it is because of this that these evils have come upon me; and behold, I am perishing of deep grief in a strange land."

After appointing Philip as regent for Antiochus V, Antiochus IV died.

In 1 Maccabees 6 the temple robbing in Persia is not the cause of Antiochus's death at all. Rather his death was the result of his arrogance toward the Jerusalem temple. Before he died, Antiochus recognized this fact and even heard about the dedication of the temple by Judas and his companions.

The five versions of Antiochus IV's death analyzed thus far have some relation to one another: They all mention his temple robbing in Persia and his final illness. Daniel 11:40-45 contains a very different account—a prophecy of Antiochus IV's miserable death in the land of Israel. It must have been written before Antiochus's death in 164 B.C. After describing various military undertakings (all in the future from the writer's perspective), the text (11:45) refers to the death of Antiochus IV: "And he shall pitch his palatial tents between the sea and the glorious holy mountain; yet he shall come to his end, with none to help him." The "glorious holy mountain" must be Mount Zion in Jerusalem (see Psalm 2:6), just as the "glorious land" (11:41) must be land of Israel. Therefore the visionary places the death of Antiochus in the land of Israel. No mention is made of the dedication of the Jerusalem temple, because from the visionary's perspective it has not yet happened.

What are we to make out of these six different accounts— four biblical and two extrabiblical—of the death of Antiochus IV? Where did he die? Was it at Tabae in Persia (Polybius), or at the temple of Nanea in Persia (2 Macc 1:13-18), or on the way from Ecbatana to Jerusalem (2 Macc 9:1-29), or at Babylon (1 Macc 6:1-16), or in the land of Israel (Dan 11:45)? When did he die? Was it after or before the dedication of the Jerusalem temple (1 Macc 6:1-16 versus 2 Macc 9:1-29)? Why did he die? Was it due to "divine" displeasure at his attempt to rob the temple of Artemis (Polybius), or in the midst of robbing the temple of Nanea (2 Macc 1:13-18), or because of his arrogance toward the Jerusalem temple (2 Macc 9:1-29; 1 Macc 6:1-16)?

What really happened? The abundance of sources makes answering that question quite difficult. If only one source existed, we would probably be satisfied with it as the answer to our questions. The presence of multiple sources describing the same event makes our task even more challenging.

One way toward understanding what is going on with these sources had been opened up from the publication of a Babylonian king list by A.J. Sachs and D.J. Wiseman in *Iraq* 16 (1954) 202-211. It states that news of the death of Antiochus IV reached Babylon between 19 November and 19 December of 164 B.C.: "Year 148, month IX, it was heard that King Antiochus died." This text indicates that Antiochus died outside of Babylon about the same time as (but probably shortly before) the dedication of the Jerusalem temple. That Antiochus IV went on a temple-robbing expedition in Persia is entirely likely. Hellenistic kings like Antiochus always needed more money to pay their soldiers and to finance their military operations in the hope of expanding their power. Just as the Jerusalem temple also served as a treasury or bank (see 2 Maccabees 3), so did other temples in the ancient world. This fact made them attractive targets for money-hungry kings.

The basic fact of Antiochus IV's death was that he died in connection with an attempt to rob a temple. The nonbiblical accounts say that it was the temple of Artemis (Polybius) or Venus (Appian); even 2 Macc 1:13-18 has Nanea. The main text of 2 Maccabees (9:1-29) and 1 Maccabees (6:1-16) sought to connect the death of Antiochus IV with the temple of the God of Israel at Jerusalem. The death of Antiochus and the dedication of the Jerusalem temple occurred at almost the very same time. Given the state of communication at the time, it is unlikely that either the Jews knew about the death of Antiochus IV before the dedication or that Antiochus IV knew about the events in Jerusalem before his death. Both writers wanted to insist that Antiochus IV died for his sins against the Jerusalem temple, the temple of Israel's God. The scenario in Dan 11:45 is unfulfilled prophecy, written before the death of Antiochus IV.

Defeat of Nicanor

A third set of problems for the historian arises from the parallels between 1 Maccabees 1—7 and 2 Maccabees 4—15. In these chapters the two books clearly tell the same basic story about the threat facing the Jews and their response under the leadership of Judas Maccabeus. Beyond the basic story, however, there are some surprising contradictions. For example, the death of Antiochus IV takes place before the dedication of the temple according to 2 Maccabees and after it according to 1 Maccabees. Even where the books tell the same story (as in the defeat of Nicanor) there are striking differences between them.

How are these differences to be explained? According to Goldstein, 2 Maccabees should be taken as a later and purposeful contradiction to 1 Maccabees in historical details and theological outlook. In other words, the author of 2 Maccabees had access to 1 Maccabees and deliberately set out to contradict it. Other solutions are possible. For example, the two authors could have used a common source to describe the events and modified that source according to their own perspectives. Or they could simply have known the story in general outline and told it rather freely. The quest for sources is complicated by the language situation and composition history of these works. 1 Maccabees seems to be the Greek translation of a (now lost) Hebrew original, and 2 Maccabees is a digest of the five-volume work of Jason of Cyrene.

At first sight the relation between 1 Maccabees and 2 Maccabees appears similar to other "synoptic" problems in biblical studies. To study the first three Gospels one customarily arranges parallel accounts in Matthew, Mark, and Luke. Most New Testament scholars conclude from such comparisons that Matthew and Luke used Mark independently. To study the relation between 1-2 Samuel and 1-2 Kings on the one hand and the books of Chronicles on the other, it is customary to arrange the parallel accounts and to trace how the Chronicler has modified his sources. The comparison of 1 Maccabees and 2 Maccabees is somewhat more complicated than those two exercises are. It is closer to the cases in the Pentateuch where one has in J (Yahweh) and E (Elohist) material two versions of the same story. Another biblical analogy is the relation between the Synoptic Gospels and John where they tell the same basic story in quite different ways. It is conceivable that one writing used the other as a source or both used a common source. But I doubt that either hypothesis can be proved.

The story of Judas's defeat of Nicanor in 1 Maccabees 7 and 2 Maccabees 14—15 is a promising place to test out the relationship between the two books. The story is told at great length in both works, and there are clear parallels between the accounts. Each narrative has a long section not found in the other: the treachery of Alcimus the high priest toward the Hasideans (1 Macc 7:8-25), and the stories of Razis's suicide (2 Macc 14:37-46) and Judas's dream-vision about his imminent battle with Nicanor (2 Macc 15:1-19). But the main story is the same in both versions: the accession of Demetrius I (1 Macc 7:1-4; 2 Macc 14:1-2), Alcimus's accusations against Judas (1 Macc 7:5-7; 2 Macc 14:3-10), Nicanor's dealings with Judas in Jerusalem (1 Macc 7:26-32; 2 Macc 14:11-30), Nicanor's threat against the temple (1 Macc 7:33-38; 2 Macc 14:31-36), and Judas's victory over Nicanor (1 Macc 7:39-50; 2 Macc 15:20-36). Examination of a few of these parallels may help us to understand what can and cannot be said about the relationship between the books as wholes.

Both books contain a brief account of the accession of Demetrius I:

1 Maccabees 7:1-4	*2 Maccabees 14:1-2*
[1]In the one hundred and fifty-first year Demetrius the son of Seleucus set forth from Rome, sailed with a few men to a city by the sea, and there began to reign. [2]As he was entering the royal palace of his fathers, the army seized Antiochus and Lysias to bring them to him. [3]But when this act became known to him, he said, "Do not let me see their faces!" [4]So the army killed them, and Demetrius took his seat upon the throne of his kingdom.	[1]Three years later, word came to Judas and his men that Demetrius, the son of Seleucus, had sailed into the harbor of Tripolis with a strong army and a fleet, [2]and had taken possession of the country, having made away with Antiochus and his guardian Lysias.

The two accounts agree in telling about the return of Demetrius I, the murder of Antiochus V and Lysias, and the accession of Demetrius I. They differ in their description of the force that accompanied Demetrius: "with a few men" (1 Macc 7:1), or "with a strong army and a fleet" (2 Macc 14:1). In a reversal of their usual literary practices, the story in 1 Maccabees is vivid and horrifying, whereas the version in 2 Maccabees is factual and flat. The pronounced differences in style and wording (even more obvious in the Greek texts) make it difficult to argue that one used the other as a source or that both used a common source.

The story of Nicanor's dealings with Judas in Jerusalem is told quite differently in 1 Macc 7:26-32 and 2 Maccabees 14:11-30. They agree that Demetrius I sent Nicanor to Jerusalem, that there seemed to be a peaceful relationship between Nicanor and Judas, and that Nicanor attempted to arrest Judas. But there are striking differences: According to 1 Macc 7:26-32, Nicanor hated and detested Israel from the start (7:26), his overtures toward peace were deceitful (7:27-28) and merely part of a scheme to seize Judas (7:29-30), and Judas

defeated Nicanor near Capharsalama (7:31-32). According to
2 Macc 14:11-30, there was an initial battle at Dessau and a
defeat for Simon (14:15-17), followed by a genuine peace and
friendship between Judas and Nicanor (14:18-25) in which
Nicanor served as a kind of mentor for Judas. Only when
Alcimus reported their friendship to Demetrius I who in turn
ordered Nicanor to arrest Judas, did Nicanor become involved
in trying to seize Judas (14:26-30).

Was Nicanor a real friend to Judas (2 Maccabees), or was he
only pretending to be a friend (1 Maccabees)? That is the chief
difference between the two accounts. One could argue that,
since Nicanor was remembered as an enemy of Israel, no one
would invent a story about his close friendship with Judas
unless it was true. Therefore the account in 2 Maccabees would
seem plausible from the historian's perspective. On the other
hand, it is just as possible that both writers knew something
about the alleged friendship between Judas and Nicanor and
interpreted that rumor in opposing ways—either as a sham (1
Maccabees), or as genuine (2 Maccabees). At any rate, there is
a major contradiction between the two works at this point.

A third test-case is found in the accounts of Judas's defeat of
Nicanor (1 Macc 7:39-50; 2 Macc 15:20-36). In both accounts
Judas prays before battle:

1 Macc 7:41-42	*2 Macc 15:22-24*
[41]"When the messengers from the king spoke blasphemy, thy angel went forth and struck down one hundred and eighty-five thousand of the Assyrians. [42]So also crush this army before us today; let the rest learn that Nicanor has spoken wickedly against thy sanctuary, and judge him according to this wickedness."	"O Lord, thou didst send thy angel in the time of Hezekiah king of Judea, and he slew fully a hundred and eighty-five thousand in the camp of Sennacherib. [23]So now, O Sovereign of the heavens, send a good angel to carry terror and trembling before us. [24]By the might of thy arm may these blasphemers who come against thy holy people be struck down."

The content of the prayers is quite similar, though the wording
is not (again the difference in Greek is more pronounced). The

rest of the story in both versions presents a common outline: Judas and Nicanor meet in battle (1 Macc 7:43a; 2 Macc 15:25-27); Judas gains victory over Nicanor and his army (1 Macc 7:43b-46; 2 Macc 15:28-29); the Jews cut off Nicanor's head and right arm, and display them publicly (1 Macc 7:47; 2 Macc 15:30-35); and they decree that the victory over Nicanor be celebrated every year on the thirteenth of Adar (1 Macc 7:48-49; 2 Macc 15:36). But once more the similarity in outline can be deceptive, for when we examine the texts more closely, we see differences:

1 Macc 7:47:

> [47]Then the Jews seized the spoils and the plunder, and they cut off Nicanor's head and the right hand which he had so arrogantly stretched out, and brought them and displayed them just outside Jerusalem.

2 Macc 15:30-35:

> [30]And the man who was ever in body and soul the defender of his fellow citizens, the man who maintained his youthful good will toward his countrymen, ordered them to cut off Nicanor's head and arm and carry them to Jerusalem. [31]And when he arrived there and had called his countrymen together and stationed the priests before the altar, he sent for those who were in the citadel. [32]He showed them the vile Nicanor's head and that profane man's arm, which had been boastfuly stretched out against the holy house of the Almighty; [33]and he cut out the tongue of the ungodly Nicanor and said that he would give it piecemeal to the birds and hang up these rewards of his folly opposite the sanctuary. [34]And they all, looking to heaven, blessed the Lord who had manifested himself, saying, "Blessed is he who has kept his own place undefiled." [35]And he hung Nicanor's head from the citadel, a clear and conspicuous sign to everyone of the help of the Lord.

The account in 1 Maccabees is crisp and informative, whereas the story in 2 Maccabees is much longer and more personal (since Judas takes the lead). In 2 Maccabees, Judas gives the order to cut off the head and arm of Nicanor (his former friend!), and then cuts out his tongue. The people respond with a prayer in praise of God: "Blessed is he who has kept his own place undefiled." According to 1 Maccabees Nicanor's head and arm were displayed just outside Jerusalem, while according to 2 Maccabees his head was hung from the citadel (15:35). What are we to make out of the parallel accounts in 1 Maccabees and 2 Maccabees? In my opinion there are too many obstacles in the way of any theory of direct dependence (one book depends directly on the other) or independent use of a common source (both used a now lost source). The chief obstacle is the way in which the books took their present form: The Greek version of 1 Maccabees is a translation of a lost Hebrew original, and the Greek text of 2 Maccabees is an epitome of a much longer work by Jason of Cyrene. This complicated process of transmission is a rather heavy screen through which to discern sources.

Moreover, the authors seem to have told their stories in their own distinctive styles, as our detailed comparisons of wording have shown. What emerges from this examination of the parallel accounts of Judas's defeat of Nicanor is that one writer *may* have used the other's work or both *may* have used a common source. But I doubt that either hypothesis can be proved. It is better to assume that both authors were familiar with the general outline of the story (from oral or even written sources) and told it in their own distinctive ways.

6

Related Sources

The major sources for the Maccabean revolt are Daniel, 2 Maccabees, and 1 Maccabees. They view the events leading up to the revolt or the events of the revolt itself from a particular vantage point: God's kingdom (Daniel), God's temple (2 Maccabees), and God's dynasty (1 Maccabees). There is no doubt about the subject matter of 1 Maccabees and 2 Maccabees. The book of Daniel is less straightforward but makes most sense when read in the context of the events preceding the Maccabean revolt.

There are other ancient sources that can help us understand the revolution studied in this book. For example, Josephus in his *Antiquities of the Jews* 12:241-13:214 gives an important paraphrase of 1 Maccabees 1:11-13:42. His omission of 1 Maccabees 14-16 has been explained in various ways: his copy was defective; those chapters were not originally part of the book; Josephus shifted to other sources; etc. But Josephus's use of 1 Maccabees (additions, omissions, etc.) is on the whole an indirect source, for his own primary source is a work that we already have and know—the Greek version of 1 Maccabees.

The Maccabean revolt is one of the few fixed points in the history of Second Temple Judaism. Most of the literature of Second Temple Judaism is allusive and therefore historically elusive. There are very few clear references to specific historical events in these works that can help us to date their composition. But as we have seen already, it is important to read these ancient Jewish writings against the background of their historical setting. Therefore one of the tasks undertaken by scholars in Second Temple Jewish literature is to relate these writings to historical events. Sometimes the grounds for making these connections are not very firm. And the events of the Maccabean revolt are commonly used for grounding a fairly large corpus of writings.

Rather than producing a catalogue of scholarly opinions according to which this or that work is related to the Maccabean revolt, I prefer to take three examples for which one can make a good case about their relevance to the Maccabean revolt. They are the Testament of Moses, the book of Judith, and the Qumran Habakkuk commentary. These works correspond to different phases in the revolt: the crisis, the defeat of Nicanor, and the accession of Jonathan (or Simon, or Alcimus) to the Jewish high priesthood. They also illustrate the difficulty involved in studying literary works as witnesses to events in Second Temple Jewish history.

Testament of Moses

Sometimes called the "Assumption of Moses," this work takes its rise from Deuteronomy 31-34. It is supposed to be Moses's farewell speech. In it Moses presents an overview of Israel's "future" history and ends with an apocalyptic picture of the coming of God's kingdom. It exists now in only one Latin manuscript from the fifth century A.D. The Latin version is acknowledged to be a translation from Greek, and the Greek a translation from Hebrew.

Chapters 6-7 contain some very clear historical references to Herod the Great and his sons: "And an insolent king will succeed them, who will not be of priestly stock . . . he will treat them ruthlessly, as the Egyptians treated them, for thirty-four years . . . he will produce children, who will succeed him and rule for shorter periods" (6:2-7). The text goes on to describe the Roman Varus as "a powerful king of the west" (6:8) who will conquer them. These and similar references in chapters 6-7 indicate that the work was written after the ouster of Herod Archelaus from power in Judea in A.D. 6. Nevertheless, these chapters about Herod and his sons give the impression of being intrusive in the work and thus of constituting an updated version of an earlier work.

The main part of the Testament of Moses is a survey of Israel's "future" history. That survey is based upon a pattern found in Deuteronomy 32 where Israel's history is viewed in terms of three phases: apostasy, punishment, and vindication. The Testament of Moses presents the first cycle of Israel's history in chapters 2-4: apostasy from Israel's entrance into the land until the exile, punishment through Nebuchadnezzar's capture of Jerusalem and the exile of the people to Babylon, and the partial vindication of the return from exile.

In the events prior to the Maccabean revolt the cycle has started over again. In chapter 5 Israel is described as "divided as to truth" (5:2), with its altars polluted by those "who are not priests but slaves and sons of slaves" (5:4). There are strong accusations of bribery and the warning that "retribution comes through kings who share their guilt" (5:1). Most of this language fits in well with the machinations of Jason and Menelaus, and the foreboding of intervention by Antiochus IV Epiphanes.

If chapters 6—7 are taken as a way of updating the work to the first century A.D., and one moves from chapter 5 to chapter 8, the result is the continuation of events connected with the Maccabean revolt. In this context Antiochus's intervention appears as the punishment for the people's apostasy: "He (=God) will stir up against them the king of the kings of the earth, a man who rules with great power, who will crucify those who confess their circumcision" (8:1). The two major issues concern circumcision and temple worship as 8:2-5 shows:

> And those who deny it he will torture and put in chains and imprison. And their wives will be given to the gods among the Gentiles, and their young sons will be operated on by the doctors to look as though they had not been circumcised. And others among them will suffer punishment by torture and fire and sword; and they will be forced to carry round their idols publicly, polluted things, just like the shrines that house them. And in the same way they will be forced by those who torture them to enter their inmost sanctuary and forced with goads to blaspheme and insult

the Name, and, as if that were not enough, the laws as well
by having a pig upon the altar.

All the matters described here can be found in other forms in
the descriptions of the persecution by Antiochus IV in 1
Maccabees and 2 Maccabees. The period in Second Temple
Jewish history in which they fit best is the crisis that led up to
the Maccabean revolt.

The response to the crisis in the Testament of Moses
combines elements from the martyr-theology of 2 Maccabees
and the apocalypticism of Daniel. The martyr-theology is
exemplified by the Levite Taxo and his seven sons in chapter 9.
Apart from the Testament of Moses, nothing is known about
Taxo. His story contains parallels with texts in 1 Maccabees
and 2 Maccabees: the slaughter of the pious ones who hid in
caves and were attacked on the Sabbath (1 Macc 2:29-38; 2
Macc 6:11), the brave martyrdom of the mother and her seven
sons (7:1-42), and the "suicide" of Razis (15:37-46).

In addressing his seven sons Taxo describes what has come
upon Jerusalem and Judea as "a cruel and unclean retribution
... far worse than the first" (9:2). He urges his sons to remain
faithful (9:6-7):

> Let us fast for three days; and on the fourth day let us go out
> to a cave in the country, and let us die rather than transgress
> the commandments of the Lord of lords, the God of our
> fathers. For if we do this and die, our blood will be avenged
> before the Lord.

Taxo and his sons are to die in the confidence that on account
of their fidelity their blood will be avenged.

When and how that vengeance will come about is described
in chapter 10 with its scenario for the coming of God's
kingdom. Whereas the first vindication (the return from the
exile) was only partial, this vindication will be complete. In the
process the martyrdoms of Taxo and his seven sons function as
the "trigger mechanism" for the coming of the kingdom. I use
the anachronistic and awkward expression "trigger mechanism" to indicate that according to the Testament of Moses
their deaths are more than an occasion for God to act but less

than the cause (since God brings in the kingdom).

The apocalyptic scenario in chapter 10 begins with the appearance of God's kingdom, the destruction of Satan, and Michael's avenging the enemies (10:1-2):

> And then shall his kingdom appear throughout all his creation;
> And then shall the Devil meet his end,
> And sorrow shall depart with him.
> Then shall be consecrated the angel who has been appointed chief,
> Who will immediately avenge them of their enemies.

Then after describing the signs and portents that will accompany the kingdom, the apocalypse describes the appearance of God, the punishment of the Gentiles, and the happiness of Israel (10:7-10):

> For the Most High will arise, the Eternal God alone,
> And he will appear to punish the Gentiles.
> And he will destroy all their idols.
> Then happy will you be, Israel;
> And you will trample upon their necks [and the wings of an eagle],
> For the time allotted them will have run its course.
> And God will exalt you,
> And set you in heaven above the stars,
> In the place where he dwells himself.
> And you will look from on high and see your enemies on earth,
> And you will recognize them and rejoice,
> And give thanks and confess your Creator.

The scenario is reminiscent of what we saw in Daniel 12:1-3 at the end of the long vision of "history" in Daniel 11. It too places the ultimate salvation of Israel outside the realm of human history.

There are good reasons to accept the "first edition" of the Testament of Moses as a witness to Jewish attitudes toward the events leading up to the Maccabean revolt. Those attitudes seem similar to what is found in the book of Daniel. The persons represented by the Testament of Moses were pious Jews who believed that the threat posed by Antiochus IV and his Jewish collaborators was serious and indeed terrible. Yet they refused to take up arms in revolt. They thought that the best defense was fidelity to the Torah, even to the point of martyrdom. They trusted that their martyrdoms would arouse God to action and that this action would be the coming of God's kingdom and the eternal happiness of God's people.

Judith

A different viewpoint and a different stage in the Maccabean revolt may be represented by the book of Judith. The viewpoint is activist, and the book may reflect Judas's defeat of Nicanor and the subsequent failures of the Maccabean movement.

The work is better called the "book of Holophernes and Judith." The first part focuses on the "Assyrian" king and his general (chaps. 1-7), and the second part concerns Judith (chaps. 8-16). The book is best understood as a historical novel, like Jonah, Tobit, and Esther. Its novelistic character is indicated by its description of the Babylonian king Nebuchadnezzar as ruling over the Assyrians (1:1), assisted by Persians, and attacking the Jews after their return from exile (4:3; 5:19). The king's identity as ruler of the Assyrians (1:1, 7, 11, etc.) may have been intended to support a connection with the current Syrian (Seleucid) rulers in Maccabean times.

Likewise, Judith appears to be a fictional character. The name means "Jewish woman." Her character combines features of several heroines from Israel's past: Miriam, Deborah, Jael, etc. The major motif running through the book is "the hand of a woman" (see 9:10; 13:15; 16:6). By the hand of Judith Israel is freed from its enemies. The survival of God's people comes about through the hand of a weak widow. Judith is intended to be a symbolic character who can inspire Israel to recognize that God can triumph even with a weak instrument. There may also be in Judith ("Jewish woman") a reminiscence of Judas Maccabeus ("Jewish man").

The focus of our treatment of the book of Judith will be the major characters: the Assyrian king and his general (chaps. 1—7), and the Jewish woman and her people (chaps. 8—16). Our goal is to discover what message the book may have sent out about the course of the Maccabean revolt. The date of the book's composition is not at all certain. But it does seem to be dealing with the events of the Maccabean revolt. Its message would have been most timely after the defeat of Nicanor and during the period of discouragement before Jonathan was able to achieve his political and military triumphs, that is, between 161 and 152 B.C.

The "book of Holophernes" (chaps. 1—7) features the "Assyrian" king and his general sent out to exact vengeance from the disobedient nations. It is doubtful that the author had any one king (Antiochus IV, Antiochus V, Demetrius I) or any one general in mind. Rather the king and the general are "typical" figures responsible for the Seleucid threat against Jerusalem and Judea. After describing Nebuchadnezzar and his campaign against Arphaxad (1:1-16) and reporting Nebuchadnezzar's commission of Holophernes (2:1-13), the "book of Holophernes" describes the campaign against the nations and their surrender (2:14—3:10). What Holophernes did (3:8) is reminiscent of Daniel 3 and 6:

> 8And he demolished all their shrines and cut down their sacred groves; for it had been given to him to destroy all the gods of the land, so that all nations should worship Nebuchadnezzar only, and all their tongues and tribes should call upon him as god.

The idea of the king's divinity and emperor worship may have been far from the mind of Antiochus IV and his Jewish supporters. Yet it may well have been suggested by coins that called him *epiphanēs theos* ("god manifest"). This inscription could easily have given rise to the rumor that Antiochus IV was demanding divine worship and wanted to be revered as a god.

Next in 4:1-15 the scene shifts to a terrified Israel and their preparations for war. The people are alarmed "both for Jerusalem and for the temple of the Lord their God" (4:2). The high priest Joachim asks the people of Bethulia to prevent the king's army from attacking Jerusalem, and the people engage in prayer and fasting.

When Holophernes inquires about the Jews from the Ammonite Achior, he learns that "as long as they did not sin against their God, they prospered" (5:17), and that "if there is no transgression in their nation ... their God will defend them" (5:21). The response of Holophernes is: "Who is God except Nebuchadnezzar?" (6:2). A major theme throughout the book of Judith is the struggle over who is the true god: Is it the king of "Assyria," or is it the God of Israel?

When Achior is expelled from the camp of Holophernes and handed over to the Israelites in Bethulia (6:2-21), Achior reports what awaits them in the imminent attack by Holophernes. The people's response concerns the arrogance of the enemy and their own humiliation (6:19):

> [19]"O Lord God of heaven, behold their arrogance, and have pity on the humiliation of our people, and look this day upon the faces of those who are consecrated to thee."

The "book of Holophernes" reaches its climax in chapter 7. The theme of Israel's fear (see 2:28; 4:2; 5:23) becomes even more prominent: "they were greatly terrified" (7:4); "their courage failed" (7:19); and "they were greatly depressed in the city" (7:32). The theme of the present crisis as a test of God is also developed: "the people of Israel cried to the Lord their God ... because all their enemies had surrounded them and there was no way of escape from them" (7:19). The first part of the book ends by leaving the resolution in God's hands (7:30-31).

It is possible to find in the "book of Holophernes" (Judith 1—7) themes that were most appropriate to the crisis facing Jerusalem and Judea in the days before the Maccabean revolt. The arrogant "Assyrian" emperor demands divine honors. He sends his equally arrogant general to make sure that those divine honors are granted. The people of Israel are terrified at what seems likely to befall them. Their only defense is God's mercy and their own fidelity to God's commandments. But at present there seems to be little hope of rescue.

The unlikely champion of Israel is the wise and beautiful widow Judith (8:1-8). She criticizes her fellow citizens of Bethulia for putting God to the test (8:12) and announces that what she is going to do "will go down through all generations" (8:32). Before setting out on her mission to the camp of Holophernes, she prays that the "Assyrians" may be crushed before they can defile the Jerusalem temple (9:7-8):

> [7]Behold now, the Assyrians are increased in their might; they are exalted, with their horses and riders; they glory in the strength of their foot soldiers; they trust in shield and spear, in bow and sling, and know not that thou art the Lord who crushest wars; the Lord is thy name. [8]Break their strength by thy might, and bring down their power in thy anger; for they intend to defile thy sanctuary, and to pollute the tabernacle where thy glorious name rests, and to cast down the horn of thy altar with the sword.

She asks that God crush their arrogance "by the hand of a woman" (9:10). Her prayer is based on the recognition that "thy power depends not upon numbers, nor thy might upon men of strength" (9:11). Though this idea is present in earlier biblical books (see Judg 7:2; 1 Sam 14:6), it also echoes Judas Maccabeus's encouragement of his troops before battle with the numerically superior army of Gorgias: "Do not fear their numbers or be afraid when they charge" (1 Macc 4:8). Judith's weapon is "the hand of a woman" (9:10).

Next Judith and her maid leave Bethulia (10:9-10) and arrive in the camp of the enemy. At the climax of a conversation full of ironies, Judith promises Holophernes: "Then I will lead you through the middle of Judea, till you come to Jerusalem; and I will set your throne in the midst of it" (11:19). She even suggests that Holophernes's alleged triumph will occur soon, before her food supply runs out (12:4). When she gets Holophernes in a drunken state, she cuts off his head and puts it in her food bag. Later she explains to the people that "the Lord has struck him down by the hand of a woman" (13:15). She orders that his head be hung up on the parapet of the city wall (14:1). It takes the "Assyrians" some time to recognize what had happened: "One Hebrew woman has brought disgrace upon the house of King Nebuchadnezzar" (14:18). Meanwhile the Jewish high priest and the leaders of the people hail Judith as follows (15:9-10):

> "You are the exaltation of Jerusalem, you are the great glory of Israel, you are the great pride of our nation! [10]You have done all this singlehanded; you have done great good to Israel, and God is well pleased with it. May the Almighty Lord bless you forever!" And all the people said, "So be it!"

In the victory celebration Judith's song praises God for saving the people of Israel from the "Assyrian" threat by the hand of a woman (16:4-6):

> [4]The Assyrian came down from the
>   mountains of the north;
>   he came with myriads of his
>   warriors;
> their multitude blocked up the
>   valleys,
>   their cavalry covered the hills.
> [5]He boasted that he would burn up
>   my territory,
>   and kill my young men with the
>   sword,
> and dash my infants to the
>   ground
>   and seize my children as prey,
>   and take my virgins as booty.
> [6]But the Lord Almighty has foiled
>   them
>   by the hand of a woman.

We cannot be certain that the author of Judith had in mind Judas's defeat of Nicanor. But the beheading, the public display of the head, and the celebration suggest some connection (see 1 Macc 7:47; 2 Macc 15:30-35).

The violence and deceit practiced by Judith raise ethical questions for the modern reader of the book. And well they should. Yet we ought not let our own preoccupations obscure what may have been a powerful message during the dark days of the Maccabean revolt. That message was that God can defeat the enemy with the weakest of instruments— even the hand of a woman (9:10; 13:15; 16:6).

The Qumran Habakkuk Commentary

The discovery of the Dead Sea scrolls in the late 1940s and early 1950s was a major event for students of Second Temple Judaism and Christian origins. The most important finds took place at Qumran where manuscripts had been hidden away in caves since the first century A.D. These manuscripts belonged to a Jewish religious community who lived in something like a monastery near the shores of the Dead Sea. The manuscripts included the oldest Hebrew texts of the Bible, fragments of extrabiblical works (some previously unknown), and writings that seem to have been distinctive of the group (e.g., its Community Rule).

One important category of the Qumran texts is the pesher. The word *pešer* in Hebrew means "interpretation." The Qumran pesharim are interpretations of biblical texts, in form something like a biblical commentary. The pesharim usually quote a section of Old Testament text and then give an interpretation. The chief difference from our modern commentaries concerns the nature of the exposition. Whereas modern commentators attempt to say what the text meant in its ancient setting, the Qumran commentators tried to say what it means in terms of their own community's life and history. The Qumran commentators looked on the biblical text as a set of mysteries or riddles to be resolved by reference to their community.

The best preserved and most extensive of the Qumran pesharim is the commentary on the book of Habakkuk. The text of this pesher contains the outlines of the community's attitude toward Scripture: The words of the biblical books contain mysteries revealed by God (7:1-2, 4); these mysteries refer to the history of the community (2:9-10; 7:1); and the interpretation of these mysteries was revealed to the Teacher of Righteousness and the interpreters who follow him (2:7-10; 7:4-5).

The Teacher of Righteousness appears to have been a major figure in the community at Qumran. His activities in leading the community seem to have taken place during the course of the Maccabean revolt. In fact, it is quite likely that the Teacher of Righteousness was the legitimate claimant to the high priesthood after Alcimus's death and before the accession of Jonathan to that office. He was from a priestly family, probably the son or brother of Onias III. Either he was not allowed to serve as high priest, or he served only in a limited capacity, or the record of his service has been erased. Whatever really went on during the so-called *intersacerdotium,* his claims to the high priesthood were pushed aside by Jonathan when the latter accepted the appointment to the high priesthood from Alexander Balas in 152 B.C. Then the so-called Teacher of Righteousness either joined up with or founded the community of religious dissidents at Qumran. This community was convinced that the Jerusalem temple was now in the wrong hands; they refused to accept the claims of Jonathan and the Maccabees to the high priesthood.

A major activity of the Qumran community was biblical interpretation. As we have already seen, this interpretation was carried out with reference to the community's life and history. The Qumran Habakkuk commentary contains passages in which this early history of the community is read into (or out of) the biblical text. Since our interest is the Maccabean revolt, we will focus on the chief characters: the Teacher of Righteousness, the Wicked Priest, and the Man of the Lie.

The Teacher of Righteousness may have founded the community. If he joined it after its foundation, his presence as the legitimate high priest certainly gave the movement a new importance. In the Habakkuk commentary the Teacher is described as "the priest into whose heart God put understanding to interpret all the words of his servants the prophets by whose hand God enumerated all that is going to come upon his people and upon his congregation" (2:8-10). This idea of the Teacher as the authoritative interpreter of the divine mysteries is found again in 7:4-5: "the Teacher of Righteousness, to whom God made known all the mysteries of the words of his servants the prophets."

The most famous text in the book of Habakkuk (because of Paul's use of it in Rom 1:16-17) is Hab 2:4b: "The righteous man will live by his faithfulness." The Qumran commentary interprets it in terms of the community and its Teacher. "The interpretation of it concerns all those who observe the Law in the House of Judah, whom God will save from the house of judgment on account of their tribulation and their fidelity to the Teacher of Righteousness" (8:1-3).

A second major character in the Qumran Habakkuk commentary is the Wicked Priest. In the early scholarship on the Dead Sea scrolls various identifications for this figure were offered. What emerged from the initial sifting of the evidence and the scholarly opinions was a consensus that the Wicked Priest was either Jonathan or Simon. More recent scholarship has turned to Jonathan. But some of the things said about him are reminiscent of Alcimus.

The Wicked Priest is described in a very negative way in 8:8-13. If the Wicked Priest was Jonathan or Simon, we have in the Qumran Habakkuk commentary evidence for strong religious opposition to the Maccabees, not just from Hellenizers or "lawless men."

> The interpretation of it concerns the Wicked Priest, who was called by the true name at the beginning of his course, but when he ruled in Israel, he became arrogant, abandoned God, and betrayed the statutes for the sake of wealth. He stole and amassed the wealth of the men of violence who had rebelled against God, and he took the wealth of peoples to add to himself guilty sin. And the abominable ways he pursued with every sort of unclean impurity.

The Wicked Priest is said to have "rebelled and transgressed the statutes of God, plundering many peoples" (8:16-17). Because of the injury that the Wicked Priest did to the Teacher of Righteousness "God gave (him) into the hand of his enemies to humble him with disease for annihilation in despair" (9:10-11; see 9:1-2). An especially heinous act by the Wicked Priest was his attack on the Teacher and his community on the Day of Atonement (11:4-8):

> The interpretation of it concerns the Wicked Priest, who pursued the Teacher of Righteousness—to swallow him up with his poisonous vexation—to his place of exile. And at the end of the feast, (during) the repose of the Day of Atonement, he appeared to them to swallow them up and to make them stumble on the fast day, their restful sabbath.

The Teacher's group and the Wicked Priest's group followed different calendars. So the Wicked Priest probably did not violate the Day of Atonement according to his own calendar. A parting shot against the Wicked Priest accuses him of drunkenness: "he walked in the ways of inebriety" (11:13-14). This reference is usually cited by those who identify Simon as the Wicked Priest, for he died at a drunken banquet according to 1 Maccabees 16. The final accusation is that the Wicked Priest "committed abomidable deeds and defiled God's sanctuary" in Jerusalem and "stole the wealth of the poor ones" in the cities of Judah (12:7-10).

Another figure in the Qumran Habakkuk commentary is called the Man of the Lie. Many scholars identify him with the Wicked Priest. But he may well be a third figure—a rival of the Teacher of Righteousness from within the community. This idea is suggested by the "traitors together with the Man of the Lie ... did not believe the words of the Teacher of Righteousness which were from the mouth of God" (2:1-3). That there was division in the community itself with regard to the Teacher of Righteousness is suggested by 5:9-12. The House of Absalom probably refers to a contemporary group and need not be taken as a code-name.

> The interpretation of it concerns the House of Absalom and their partisans, who were silent at the rebuke of the Teacher of Righteousness and did not support him against the Man of the Lie—who rejected the Law in the midst of all their council.

The Man of the Lie may have been the leader of the community before the Teacher joined it. Or he may have opposed the Teacher's leadership at some point. He may have even founded a rival community, as 10:10 suggests: "building a city of vanity with bloodshed and establishing a congregation with deceit."

The Qumran Habakkuk commentary provides important data about the founding of the Dead Sea community and about popular acceptance of the Maccabean revolt. It suggests that not all Israel was willing to accept Jonathan (or Simon, or Alcimus) as the high priest and leader of the people. It indicates that there was a priest around with good claims to the office of high priest—and his claims were not honored. In response to being forced out of the Jerusalem temple he joined (or founded) a sectarian group in the wilderness who were waiting for God to make things right again (as in Daniel and Testament of Moses). Through the discovery of a text lost for two-thousand years we can know more about the fascinating story of the Maccabean revolt.

7

Significance

This book is intended as an introduction to the literature and events of the Maccabean revolt. It aims to initiate nonspecialists into study of a body of difficult literature, a decisive period in ancient Jewish history, and the Hellenistic world. The book began by situating the principal literary sources for the Maccabean revolt in the canon of Scripture and in the history of Second Temple Judaism. Then it provided a guide to the stories and visions in the book of Daniel, with particular attention to their message against the background of the threat posed by Antiochus IV Epiphanes. Next it picked up the story begun in Daniel with an analysis of 2 Maccabees —that charming and often exciting collection of stories about how God and Israel's heroes defended the Jerusalem temple and preserved it from sacrilege. The last major source studied was 1 Maccabees, written in the style of biblical history and carrying on the narrative of the Maccabean revolt from Judas to Jonathan and Simon. Particular attention was given in these analyses to the distinctive angles from which each book views the events that it narrates: God's kingdom (Daniel), God's temple (2 Maccabees), and God's dynasty (1 Maccabees).

On the basis of these readings of the three primary sources, it was then possible to sketch the outlines of the so-called Maccabean revolt from beginning to end and through its high points and low points. Attention was also given to some problems facing the historian of the Maccabean revolt: the nature of the "persecution," the contradictory accounts, and the parallel accounts.

As a way of filling out the sketch of events provided by the primary sources, we showed how other sources (Testament of Moses, Judith, the Qumran Habakkuk commentary) can be read against the background of the Maccabean revolt. This exercise (and it could be repeated with other works such as Jubilees, parts of 1 Enoch, other Qumran writings, etc.) revealed further "distinctive" approaches to the events. The diversity of Second Temple Judaism is illustrated very clearly by the literature of the Maccabean revolt.

The final chapter in this introduction to the Maccabean revolt is the appropriate place to bring together by way of synthesis some of the most important ideas and themes uncovered in our presentation. Why is the Maccabean revolt significant? Why should anyone want to study it? What is so important about it?

An easy way to answer questions about the significance of the Maccabean revolt is to divide our reflections into three sections: literary, historical, and theological. These three areas obviously overlap. Nevertheless they provide a neat framework for our concluding considerations.

Literary

The events of the Maccabean revolt generated the three major sources (Daniel, 1—2 Maccabees) and most likely other writings (Testament of Moses, Judith, the Qumran Habakkuk commentary, etc.). Not all were written at the same time. Some seem even to have been written at a distance from the events that they describe. Yet it is fair to say that the Maccabean revolt was the occasion for an outpouring of literature. These were important events, and people felt deeply about them.

The literature of the Maccabean revolt is striking for its variety of literary genres. The most prominent and influential genre is the apocalypse represented by Daniel and the Testament of Moses. Both books contain visions of Israel's "future history" that climax with the coming of God's kingdom. Though not necessarily the earliest apocalypse, Daniel surely has had the greatest impact in both Judaism and

Christianity. The apocalypse represents the longing of people for a new and better world when they seemed most powerless to change the present world. It was the ideal vehicle for pious people without military might and armed only with trust in God's fidelity to the promises made to Israel.

First and Second Maccabees are clearly "history" books. Though they may not meet the standards of nineteenth- and twentieth-century historians, in the ancient world they would easily be recognized as historical accounts. They share the ancient historian's fondness for military actions, for moral examples, and for appropriate speeches placed on the lips of their heroes.

Second Maccabees is sometimes described as "pathetic history" on the grounds that its mode of storytelling seeks to stir up the passions (*pathē*) and get the reader involved on an emotional level. Though there is some doubt that "pathetic history" really was a literary genre in antiquity, the expression does at least describe the emotional character of the story told in 2 Maccabees.

First Maccabees is usually called "dynastic history." It is the story of a Jewish dynasty from Mattathias, through Judas, Jonathan, and Simon, down to John Hyrcanus. While retaining some of the conventions of Hellenistic historiography, 1 Maccabees is "biblical" in style. Its language, use of prayers, and spirit indicate that the author took as models the earlier historical books of the Bible. Thus part of its "propaganda" was the suggestion that the Maccabees carried on the biblical tradition and that their dynasty was the legitimate heir of that tradition.

The "novel" genre is represented by Judith, and the biblical "commentary" by the Qumran Habakkuk commentary. The book of Judith is quite sophisticated in its development of characters, its use of irony, its movement from scene to scene, and its control of plot. The Qumran Habakkuk commentary shows how one Jewish community read the Scriptures as fulfilled at least in part in the events of the Maccabean revolt and their own community.

The series of events that today we call the Maccabean revolt generated a variety of responses as well as a variety of ways of responding: apocalypse, pathetic history, dynastic history, novel, and biblical commentary. Though not invented during the Maccabean revolt, these literary genres were surely helped to prominence and developed by their use in connection with those events. Their influence on Jews and Christians through the centuries has been powerful.

Historical

On the historical level the sources for the Maccabean revolt are significant for the problems that they pose and the opportunities that they afford. The variety of sources gives the rare chance in either biblical studies or ancient history to look at a single series of events from several independent perspectives. As we have seen, those perspectives are quite clear and definite: God's kingdom (Daniel), God's temple (2 Maccabees), and God's dynasty (1 Maccabees). The reverse side of this blessed abundance of sources is the confusion caused by contradictions among the sources and the assumptions that guide the presentations in the sources. What really happened? To answer that question the historian must often "play detective," sifting through the sources, reading them in the light of other sources, and putting together the most likely scenario of events.

The historical importance of the Maccabean revolt is obvious. From being a client poeple in the Seleucid empire, the Jews of Palestine moved to political independence with their own native ruler and with powerful allies. From being in danger of cultural and religious extinction the Jews of Palestine moved to a form of religious life that was both traditional and adaptable to the realities of the time. In the crisis period under Jason and Menelaus the fate of Judaism (and with it Christianity and Islam) was uncertain. The result of the Maccabean revolt was a Judaism with both clear definition and flexibility. There would be no further arguments about the centrality of the Torah and the Jerusalem temple. Their place within Judaism was settled as a result of the Maccabean revolt.

The sources for the Maccabean revolt also show how Israel related to other peoples. Since the late fourth century B.C.

(under Alexander the Great) Israel had been part of that larger entity called Hellenism. Study of Maccabean sources opens up the Hellenistic world with its dynastic struggles between the Ptolemies and the Seleucids. The people of Israel found themselves between two greater powers; their fortunes coincided with the rise and fall of the Ptolemaic and Seleucid rulers. The Jewish alliances with Rome illustrate how in the third and second centuries B.C. Rome extended its influence in the East and set the stage for more direct rule in the first century.

Jewish history in the Maccabean period gives an important glimpse of life in the Hellenistic world. Native peoples like the Jews found themselves in the middle of battles between powerful kings. They came to use the Greek language and Greek techniques in economics, warfare, and government. Yet they struggled to retain their native heritage in language, religion, and culture. The tensions for these peoples were severe, and very few survived with such clarity and vitality as the Jews of Palestine did.

The Maccabean revolt is also significant for historians of revolutions. No two revolutions are quite the same. Nevertheless it is possible to discern similarities, to pick out patterns, and to make predictions on the basis of these patterns. From the case of the Maccabean revolt some interesting lessons can be learned: There was a difference between the initial goal (getting rid of the objectionable kind of worship in the Jerusalem temple) and the ultimate goal that was achieved (political independence for the Jews). The course of the revolution was anything but straight; there were times when all seemed lost, and only when Jonathan joined political skill to military endeavors was success achieved. Despite 1 Maccabees (and the picture that has come down to us in the history books) there was no unanimity among Jews and a good deal of opposition to the Maccabees from both the pious and the "lawless." The Maccabean revolt was a "biblical revolution" in the sense that its major characters patterned their actions on biblical examples, encouraged their followers by appealing to biblical precedents, and restored a form of worship based on the statutes of Scripture.

Theological

The theological influence of the book of Daniel in particular and of Jewish apocalypticism in general on early Christianity should be obvious. Jesus's prayer "thy kingdom come" expresses the longing of Jews and Christians for the coming of God's kingdom as in Daniel and other apocalyptic writings. The major theme of Jesus's teachings in parables and other forms was the kingdom of God—an idea that took its apocalyptic shape during the crisis that eventuated in the Maccabean revolt. Apocalypticism provided many of the theological terms and concepts for Jesus and the early Christians—so much so that apocalyptic has been called the "mother of Christian theology."

Besides the kingdom of God, Jewish apocalypticism also supplied familiar Christian notions like "Son of Man" and resurrection. The Son of Man sayings in the Gospel tradition divide into three classes: those about Jesus in the present, those spoken in predictions of the passion and resurrection, and those that refer to a future figure (e.g., "you will see the Son of Man seated at the right hand of Power and coming with the clouds of heaven," Mk 14:62). There is no doubt about a connection between Daniel 7 and the third class of Son of Man sayings. The debate in New Testament scholarship concerns only whether Jesus spoke this way about himself and the connection of the first two classes of sayings with the third class.

Resurrection was originally part of the complex of beliefs that make up Jewish apocalypticism. In fact, the resurrection of the dead is one element in the Jewish scenario of events that are to accompany the full coming of God's kingdom. What is so unusual about Christian belief in Jesus's resurrection is the claim that in this one case the fullness of God's kingdom has been anticipated! That is what Jews find so hard to accept. Though it may be possible to find allusions to resurrection in some earlier biblical books, there can be no doubt about its prominence in Daniel 12 and 2 Maccabees 7. Some scholars view Jewish belief in the resurrection as a response to Greek ideas about the immortality of the soul. Whatever the early history of the doctrine may have been, it surely came to prominence in Judaism in connection with the Maccabean revolt and came to Christianity through Judaism.

Another apocalyptic element from the book of Daniel that made its way into early Christianity is the so-called "abomination of desolation" (see Dan 11:31; 12:11; Mk 13:14 parr.): "But when you see the desolating sacrilege set up where it ought not to be (let the reader understand), then let those who are in Judea flee to the mountains." In the book of Daniel the expression describes the "sacred stones" placed on the altar in the Jerusalem temple in 167 B.C. The expression was a savage word-play on the divine epithet "Baal Shamin" ("Lord of Heaven"). By New Testament times the expression had taken on a life of its own and could be used in the so-called Synoptic apocalypse (Mark 13 parr.) as part of a code describing events preceding the coming of God's kingdom in its fullness.

The theological influence of 1 Maccabees and 2 Maccabees is not nearly so dramatic as that of Daniel has been. While there may be a few vague allusions to these books in the New Testament, there are no direct references to them. Nevertheless, these books have exercised a powerful influence on Jewish and Christian behavior through the centuries. They have provided models for both martyrs and rebels.

The models for martyrs appear mainly in 2 Maccabees, especially the story of the mother and her seven sons (chap. 7). The Maccabean martyrs hold firm to their religious principles. They refuse to compromise their beliefs even under the threat of torture and death. They go to their death with the conviction that in the resurrection of the dead they will be vindicated and their persecutors brought to divine justice.

Another kind of model is provided by Mattathias, Judas, Jonathan, and Simon. These are the rebels against unjust governments, the guerrilla warriors, the men of action, the practical ones who know how to increase their power. Standing even more firmly in the biblical tradition than the martyrs do, these models of this-wordly activism have provided the example for champions of religious freedom and national independence through the centuries. With the emergence of the modern state of Israel there has been a remarkable shift in consciousness about heroes among many Jews. Whereas in the past the heroes of Judaism have been the wise scholars or sages, now men of action like David and the Maccabees are gaining favor.

There has been, however, a puzzling ambivalence regarding the Maccabean revolt in the Jewish tradition. The feast of Hanukkah has been celebrated through the years. Yet despite its prominence in some parts of the world (because of its proximity to Christmas), it is regarded as a minor festival. More puzzling is the disappearance of the Hebrew original of 1 Maccabees from the canon of Hebrew Scriptures. These puzzlements lead scholars to suspect that at some point in the first century there was a Jewish reaction against the Maccabees and what they stood for, and a deliberate attempt to push them out of the sacred tradition of Judaism. Perhaps "messianic" claims were being made about Judas Maccabeus or some other figure who traced his ancestry back to the Maccabean movement. Perhaps in light of failed uprisings against the Romans by Jews claiming to follow the example of Judas and his brothers, the custodians of Judaism came to regard the Maccabees as too controversial and too dangerous.

The "messianic" dimension to the Maccabean movement may be reflected in the only New Testament episode that is explicitly tied to Hanukkah (John 10:22-39). The evangelist goes to some effort to set the debate between Jesus and his Jewish opponents at Hanukkah: "It was the feast of the Dedication at Jerusalem; it was winter, and Jesus was walking in the temple, in the portico of Solomon" (10:22-23). The first question put to Jesus concerns his "messianic" identity: "If you are the Christ, tell us plainly" (10:24). When Jesus goes beyond the terms of the question and proclaims that "I and the Father are one" (10:30), his opponents accuse him of blasphemy "because you, being a man, make yourself God" (10:33). In his discourse Jesus claims to be able to give to his flock "eternal life, and they shall never perish, and no one shall snatch them out of my hand" (10:28). His claim to be able to give eternal life is illustrated by the Lazarus story (John 11), which immediately follows the Hanukkah episode.

The question about Jesus's identity as messiah, the charge that he makes himself God, and the emphasis on the theme of eternal life—all these themes suggest that the Hanukkah setting for this episode is not accidental. Rather, the incident appears to be part of John's effort in the "Book of Signs" (John 1—12) to show that in Jesus Jewish feasts and institutions reach their fullness.

These concluding reflections about the literary, historical, and theological significance of the Maccabean revolt are intended only as a way of bringing together some themes that have emerged in the course of our study. Since the goal of this book is to initiate its readers into the fascinating story of the Maccabean revolt and to indicate its significance, I have included an annotated bibliography of modern scholarly resources that I have found helpful. My hope is that this book will enable you to use them wisely and profitably.

Annotated Bibliography

Principal Sources

F.-M. Abel, *Les Livres des Maccabées* (Etudes Bibliques; Paris: Gabalda, 1949). This classic scholarly commentary on 1—2 Maccabees is especially important because of its author's mastery of Greek grammar and Palestinian geography.

John R. Bartlett, *The First and Second Books of Maccabees* (Cambridge Bible Commentary: New English Bible; Cambridge, UK—London—New York: Cambridge University Press, 1973). Bartlett's introductions and notes convey important information clearly and concisely.

John J. Collins, *Daniel, First Maccabees, Second Maccabees* (Old Testament Message 16; Wilmington, DE: Michael Glazier, 1981). This exposition of the RSV text gives particular attention to the problem of war as it arises from 1—2 Maccabees; it also contains an excursus on the apocalyptic genre.

John C. Dancy, *A Commentary on I Maccabees* (Oxford: Basil Blackwell, 1954). This introduction to and commentary on 1 Maccabees relies on the scholarly work of Edwyn Bevan, Elias Bickerman, and F.-M. Abel. Though now somewhat dated, it remains a helpful commentary for its clarity, framing of issues, and sound critical judgments.

Robert Doran, *Temple Propaganda: The Purpose and Character of 2 Maccabees* (Catholic Biblical Quarterly Monograph Series 12; Washington, DC: Catholic Biblical Association, 1981). In addition to analyzing 2 Maccabees as temple propaganda, the volume shows how the work provided its readers with the proper perspective from which to assess their leaders.

Agneta Enermalm-Ogawa, *Un langage de prière juif en grec: Le témoignage des deux premiers livres des Maccabées* (Stockholm: Almqvist & Wiksell, 1987). This literary and linguistic analysis of prayers in 1 and 2 Maccabees seeks to discover their functions in the books in which they appear and to contribute to understanding the language of Jewish prayer in Greek.

Jonathan A. Goldstein, *I Maccabees. A New Translation with Introduction and Commentary* (Anchor Bible 41; Garden City, NY: Doubleday, 1976); *II Maccabees. A New Translation with Introduction and Commentary* (Anchor Bible 41A; Garden City, NY: Doubleday, 1983). The most up-to-date and extensive treatments of the books of Maccabees, these books are encyclopedic and often complicated. On some issues Goldstein changed his mind in the second volume. See chapter 5 of this book for a discussion of some of Goldstein's views.

Louis F. Hartman and Alexander A. Di Lella, *The Book of Daniel. A New Translation with Introduction, Notes, and Commentary* (Anchor Bible 23; Garden City, NY: Doubleday, 1978). Hartman did the commentary on chapters 1—9, and Di Lella did the rest after Hartman's death. Di Lella also provided a 124-page introduction.

Nils Martola, *Capture and Liberation. A Study in the Composition of the First Book of Maccabees* (Acta Academiae Aboensis, Ser. A: Humaniora 63.1; Åbo, Finland: Åbo Akademi, 1984). This literary-critical investigation of 1 Maccabees contains analytic and synthetic sections, and shows that the theme of the main story was capture and liberation.

James A. Montgomery, *A Critical and Exegetical Commentary on the Book of Daniel* (International Critical Commentary 22; Edinburgh: T. & T. Clark, 1927). One of the truly great biblical commentaries, this volume is still valuable for its information on philological and textual matters.

Sidney Tedesche and Solomon Zeitlin, *The First Book of Maccabees* (Jewish Apocryphal Literature; New York: Harper & Brothers, 1950); *The Second Book of Maccabees* (1954). These volumes present on facing pages the Greek text and an English translation, with extensive notes below. Zeitlin's thesis about the lateness of the last three chapters of 1 Maccabees has not found scholarly support.

History of the Maccabean Revolt

Elias Bickerman, *The God of the Maccabees. Studies on the Meaning and Origin of the Maccabean Revolt* (Studies in Judaism and Late Antiquity 32; Leiden: Brill, 1979). The major scholarly monograph on the historical background of Antiochus IV's intervention in the affairs of Jerusalem. See the discussion in chapter 5 of this book.

_____, *Studies in Jewish and Christian History. Part Two* (Arbeiten zur Geschichte des antiken Judentums und des Urchristentums 9; Leiden: Brill, 1980). The sixteen articles in this second of four volumes of Bickerman's collected essays concern issues pertaining to the Maccabean revolt, thus serving as an important supplement to *The God of the Maccabees*.

Klaus Bringmann, *Hellenistische Reform und Religionsverfolgung in Judäa. Eine Untersuchung zur jüdisch-hellenistische Geschichte (175-163 v. Chr.)* (Abhandlungen der Akademie der Wissenschaften, Philologisch-Historisch Klasse, Dritte Folge 132; Göttingen: Vandenhocck & Ruprecht, 1983). A fresh interpretation of the Antiochan crisis in Jerusalem, with particular emphasis on political and economic factors. See chapter 5 of this book for a discussion.

Otto Mørkholm, *Antiochus IV of Syria* (Classica et Mediaevalia, Dissertationes 8; Copenhagen: Gyldendalske Boghandel, 1966). A collection of ancient evidence pertaining to Antiochus IV Epiphanes along with interpretations of it.

E. Nodet, "La Dédicace, les Maccabées et le Messie," *Revue Biblique* 93 (1986) 321-375. The four parts of this extraordinarily rich article deal with the Maccabees and the institution of Hanukkah, Josephus' accounts of Hanukkah and the temple of Onias, Hanukkah in rabbinic sources, and the warrior messiah and the Mishnah.

Moshe Pearlman, *The Maccabees* (London—Jerusalem: Weidenfeld and Nicolson, 1973). An interpretation of Daniel and 1—2 Maccabees as prefiguring the modern state of Israel. Though not a work of critical scholarship, it is written in an engaging way and is well illustrated.

Viktor Tcherikover, *Hellenistic Civilization and the Jews* (Philadelphia: Jewish Publication Society, 1961). Bringing to bear a remarkable knowledge of the pertinent documents, Tcherikover provides an exciting synthesis of his views on Jewish history. See chapter 5 of this volume for a discussion of his views.

Related Jewish Writings

James H. Charlesworth (ed.), *The Old Testament Pseudepigrapha* (2 vols.; Garden City, NY: Doubleday, 1983, 1985). These volumes contain introductions to and annotated translations of over fifty Jewish writings from the Second Temple period, including some works customarily dated to the Maccabean period.

Toni Craven, *Artistry and Faith in the Book of Judith* (SBL Dissertation Series 70; Chico, CA: Scholars Press, 1983). This literary analysis of the book of Judith is especially effective in establishing the book's outline and in illumining the construction of individual units.

Frank M. Cross, *The Ancient Library of Qumran and Modern Biblical Studies* (rev. ed.; Garden City, NY: Doubleday, 1961). Now over thirty years old from its first edition, this introduction to the Dead Sea scrolls remains the best book on the topic.

Maurya P. Horgan, *Pesharim: Qumran Interpretation of Biblical Books* (Catholic Biblical Quarterly Monograph Series 8; Washington, DC: Catholic Biblical Association, 1979). The most extensive philological commentary on the Pesharim. The translations of the Qumran Habakkuk commentary in chapter 6 follow Horgan's translation.

Robert A. Kraft and George W.E. Nickelsburg (eds.), *Early Judaism and Its Modern Interpreters* (Atlanta: Scholars Press, 1986; Philadelphia: Fortress). The seventeen essays in this volume provide the current state of scholarship on various issues in Second Temple Judaism and extensive bibliographies.

George W.E. Nickelsburg, *Jewish Literature Between the Bible and the Mishnah. A Historical and Literary Introduction* (Philadelphia: Fortress, 1981). The great strength of this introduction to the Old Testament Apocrypha and Pseudepigrapha (and the Qumran scrolls) is that it ties the literature to historical events and movements, such as the Maccabean revolt.

H.F.D. Sparks (ed.), *The Apocryphal Old Testament* (Oxford: Clarendon, 1985). A collection of twenty-five Jewish writings from the Second Temple period, with introductions and notes.

Michael E. Stone (ed.), *Jewish Writings of the Second Temple Period: Apocrypha, Pseudepigrapha, Qumran Sectarian Writings, Philo, Josephus* (Compendia 2.2;

Assen: Van Gorcum, 1984; Philadelphia: Fortress).
An excellent introduction to Jewish literature after the
Hebrew Bible and not part of the rabbinic corpus

Geza Vermes, *The Dead Sea Scrolls. Qumran in Perspective*
(Cleveland: Collins & World, 1978; Philadelphia:
Fortress). A synthesis of modern scholarship on the
Dead Sea scrolls.

Jewish History in the Hellenistic Age

Elias Bickerman, *From Ezra to the Last of the Maccabees.
Foundations of Post-Biblical Judaism* (New York:
Schocken, 1962). This simple presentation of Second
Temple Judaism by a master scholar is an excellent
introduction to the period.

Shaye J.D. Cohen, *From the Maccabees to the Mishnah*
(Library of Early Christianity 7; Philadelphia: Westminster, 1987). A bold synthesis of scholarship on
Jewish history and religion in the Second Temple
period.

Martin Hengel, *Jews, Greeks and Barbarians. Aspects of the
Hellenization of Judaism in the pre-Christian Period*
(Philadelphia: Fortress, 1980). This volume treats the
political and social history of Palestine from Alexander
to Antiochus III, aspects of the Hellenization of
Judaism, and the encounter between Judaism and
Hellenism in the Diaspora and Palestine.

—————, *Judaism and Hellenism. Studies in their
Encounter in Palestine during the Early Hellenistic
Period* (2 vols.; Philadelphia: Fortress, 1974). A major
synthesis of scholarship on the encounter between
Judaism and Hellenism with respect to (1) political,
military, and socioeconomic developments, (2) Greek
language, names, education, and literature, (3) religious
and theological questions, and (4) the early Greek
descriptions of Judaism and the Jewish attempt at
reform in Jerusalem.

Abraham Schalit (ed.), *The Hellenistic Age. Political History of Jewish Palestine from 332 B.C.E. to 67 B.C.E.* (World History of the Jewish People. First Series: Ancient Times, vol. 6; Jerusalem: Masada Publishing, 1972; New Brunswick, NJ: Rutgers University Press). This history of the Jewish people from the fourth to the first century B.C. features contributions by M. Avi-Yonah, J. Klausner, Tcherikover, and Schalit.

Emil Schürer, *The History of the Jewish People in the Age of Jesus Christ (175 B.C.-A.D. 135)* (rev. and ed. by Geza Vermes and Fergus Millar; Edinburgh: T. & T. Clark, 1973-87; Philadelphia: Fortress). The updated and revised version of Schürer's classic handbook on Second Temple Judaism provides important historical data.

The Hellenistic World

M.M. Austin (ed.), *The Hellenistic world from Alexander to the Roman conquest. A selection of ancient sources in translation* (Cambridge, UK—London—New York: Cambridge University Press, 1981). The 279 ancient texts in this anthology illustrate the main lines in the development of the Hellenistic states, their institutions, society, and economy. The collection allows one to locate the Maccabean revolt in its Hellenistic context.

Henry Bettenson (trans.), *Livy: Rome and the Mediterranean* (New York: Penguin, 1976). The English version of books 31 through 45 in Livy's history of Rome provides important background material for developments in Mediterranean history from 200 to 167 B.C.

Alan K. Bowman, *Egypt after the Pharaohs. 332 BC-AD 642 from Alexander to the Arab Conquest* (Berkeley, CA: University of California Press, 1986). A beautifully illustrated survey of Egyptian history in Ptolemaic, Roman, and Byzantine periods.

Samuel K. Eddy, *The King Is Dead. Studies in the Near Eastern Resistance to Hellenism 334-31 B.C.* (Lincoln, NB: University of Nebraska Press, 1961). By examining the ways in which various peoples (including the Jews) reacted to Hellenism, Eddy also shows how the native cultures were both transformed and preserved.

Erich S. Gruen, *The Hellenistic World and the Coming of Rome* (2 vols.; Berkeley, CA—Los Angeles—London: University of California Press, 1984). A survey of Roman expansion in the East during the third and second centuries B.C. against the background of Greek society and institutions.

Arnaldo Momigliano, *Alien Wisdom. The Limits of Hellenization* (Cambridge, UK—London—New York—Melbourne: Cambridge University Press, 1975). A distinguished historian of antiquity discusses the cultural connections between Greeks, Romans, Celts, Jews, and Persians in the Hellenistic period—especially how the Greeks came to know and evaluate non-Greeks in relation to their own civilization.

Michael Rostovtzeff, *The Social and Economic History of the Hellenistic World* (3 vols., 2nd ed.; Oxford: Clarendon Press, 1952). This massive undertaking by one of the great masters of the Hellenistic period remains the monumental study in the field.

Ian Scott-Kilvert (trans.), *Polybius: The Rise of the Roman Empire* (New York: Penguin, 1979). Polybius describes "by what means and under what system of government the Romans succeeded in less than fifty-three years (220 to 167 B.C.) in bringing under their rule almost the whole of the inhabited world, an achievement which is without parallel in human history."

William W. Tarn and G.T. Griffith, *Hellenistic Civilization* (3rd rev. ed.; Cleveland—New York: World, 1961). Tarn was one of the great authorities on Hellenism and the author of several very large books. The volume summarizes the scholarship of the previous generation.

Frank W. Walbank, *The Hellenistic World* (Cambridge, MA: Harvard University Press, 1982). An up-to-date synthesis of research on Hellenistic history and culture by an experienced specialist. In many respects it replaces the synthesis by Tarn and Griffith.

Apocalypticism

John J. Collins, *The Apocalyptic Imagination. An Introduction to the Jewish Matrix of Christianity* (New York: Crossroad, 1984). After an introduction to the apocalyptic genre, Collins surveys Jewish apocalyptic writings such as the early Enoch literature, Daniel, the Qumran documents, and related works.

Paul D. Hanson, *The Dawn of Apocalyptic. The Historical and Sociological Roots of Jewish Apocalyptic Eschatology* (rev. ed.; Philadelphia: Fortress, 1979). Hanson argues that Jewish apocalyptic eschatology developed from preexilic and exilic prophecy and that outside influences (e.g., Persian dualism and Hellenism) were late.

_____, (ed.), *Visionaries and their Apocalypses* (Issues in Religion and Theology 4; Philadelphia: Fortress, 1983). After a fifteen-page introduction, this anthology provides seven important articles on apocalyptic by leading modern scholars.

Klaus Koch, *The Rediscovery of Apocalyptic* (Studies in Biblical Theology 2.22; London: SCM, 1972). The book's subtitle expresses its thrust: "A polemical work on a neglected area of biblical studies and its damaging effects on theology and philosophy."

George W.E. Nickelsburg, *Resurrection, Immortality, and Eternal Life in Intertestamental Judaism* (Harvard Theological Studies 26; Cambridge, MA: Harvard University Press, 1972). This exegetical analysis of Jewish texts that deal with resurrection, immortality, and eternal life includes extensive treatments of Daniel 12 and 1 Maccabees 7.

D.S. Russell, *The Method and Message of Jewish Apocalyptic. 200 BC-AD 100* (Old Testament Library; Philadelphia: Westminster, 1964). This well-known introduction to Jewish apocalyptic is divided into three parts: nature and identity, method, and message.

Walter Schmithals, *The Apocalyptic Movement: Introduction and Interpretation* (Nashville: Abingdon, 1975). Both an introduction to apocalyptic literature and an interpretation of it as a way of understanding human existence.

Son of Man

Maurice Casey, *Son of Man. The interpretation and influence of Daniel 7* (London: SPCK, 1979). Casey concludes that Daniel 7 accounts for the term "Son of Man" in only a small group of New Testament sayings.

Chris C. Caragounis, *The Son of Man. Vision and Interpretation* (Wissenschaftliche Untersuchungen zum Neuen Testament 38; Tübingen: Mohr-Siebeck, 1986). According to Caragounis, the Son of Man figure was associated with God's rule from the very beginning and as earthly Son of Man Jesus understood his task to be announcing God's kingdom.

Arthur J. Ferch, *The Son of Man in Daniel 7* (Andrews University Seminary Doctoral Dissertation Series 6; Berrien Springs, MI: Andrews University, 1979). Ferch surveys interpretations of the Son of Man in Daniel, evaluates theories about the origin of and alleged parallels to the Son of Man figure, and locates the Son of Man within the literary structure of Daniel 7.

Barnabas Lindars, *Jesus Son of Man. A Fresh Examination of the Son of Man Sayings in the Gospels in the Light of Recent Research* (London: SPCK, 1983). According to Lindars, the original meaning of "Son of Man" on the lips of Jesus must be found elsewhere than in Daniel 7.

Other Books of Interest

Crane Brinton, *The Anatomy of Revolution* (rev. and expanded; New York: Vintage Books, 1965). Though not directly related to biblical studies, this examination of four modern revolutions (English, American, French, Russian) makes one sensitive to the process through which revolutions pass.

Peter C. Craigie, *The Problem of War in the Old Testament* (Grand Rapids: Eerdmans, 1979). This theological exploration of Israel's religious wars argues that war was inescapably linked to the existence of the state and to religion in the ancient Near East.

Richard A. Horsley, *Jesus and the Spiral of Violence* (San Francisco: Harper & Row, 1987). Horsley discerns four stages in the "spiral of violence": institutionalized injustice, protest and resistance, repression, and revolt. In his treatment of the Maccabean revolt he generally follows Tcherikover. He contends that Jesus was neither a violent political revolutionary nor a pacifist but rather a social revolutionary.

Michael Walzer, *Exodus and Revolution* (New York: Basic Books, 1985). Moving back and forth between the biblical accounts of the exodus and later revolutions shaped by them, Walzer shows how Pharaonic oppression, deliverance, Sinai, and Canaan remain with us as powerful memories influencing our political perceptions.